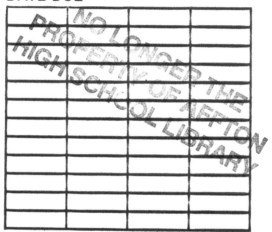
DEMCO

ISSUES THAT CONCERN YOU

School Violence

Peggy Daniels, *Book Editor*

GREENHAVEN PRESS
A part of Gale, Cengage Learning

GALE
CENGAGE Learning

Detroit • New York • San Francisco • New Haven, Conn • Waterville, Maine • London

Christine Nasso, *Publisher*
Elizabeth Des Chenes, *Managing Editor*

© 2009 Greenhaven Press, a part of Gale, Cengage Learning

For more information, contact:
Greenhaven Press
27500 Drake Rd.
Farmington Hills, MI 48331-3535
Or you can visit our Internet site at gale.cengage.com

Articles in Greenhaven Press anthologies are often edited for length to meet page requirements. In addition, original titles of these works are changed to clearly present the main thesis and to explicitly indicate the author's opinion. Every effort is made to ensure that Greenhaven Press accurately reflects the original intent of the authors. Every effort has been made to trace the owners of copyrighted material.

Cover image: MarioTama/Getty Images

LIBRARY OF CONGRESS CATALOGING-IN-PUBLICATION DATA

School violence / Peggy Daniels, book editor.
    p. cm. — (Issues that concern you)
  Includes bibliographical references and index.
  ISBN 978-0-7377-4186-5 (hardcover)
  1. School violence—United States—Juvenile literature. I. Daniels, Peggy.
  LB3013.32.S348 2009
  371.7'820973—dc22
                                                    2008043431

Printed in the United States of America
 2 3 4 5 6 7 12 11 10 09

CONTENTS

As incidents of violence in and around schools make news headlines with disturbing frequency, school violence continues to be one of the most hotly debated topics in America. Public discussion often focuses on questions that have no easy answers: What causes school violence? What can be done to prevent violence in schools? What makes schools safe? Some experts believe the large size of many modern schools is to blame, while others claim that bullying, low self-esteem, social isolation, and pressure to conform are all contributors to outbreaks of school violence. To maintain an environment that allows students to learn in a safe setting, some schools are turning to increased campus security. Others are exploring alternative prevention strategies that encourage individual responsibility, such as youth leadership programs and mentoring. These ideas, along with many other aspects of the school violence issue, are addressed in this volume.

The School Violence Problem

School violence is not a new problem. Unfortunately, for as long as schoolyards have existed, school bullies have been starting fights, stealing lunch money, and intimidating other students. Even large-scale school violence is not new. What has been called the worst incident of school violence in U.S. history occurred in 1927 in Bath Township, Michigan. In May of that year, the Bath Consolidated School was destroyed in a series of bombings that killed 45 people—38 children and 7 adults—and injured 58 more. This tragedy stunned the nation, and the story appeared on the front page of newspapers across the country. Then in April 1999 school violence once again became a national concern after the tragic events at Columbine High School in Littleton, Colorado, where 15 people were killed and another 23 were wounded in one day.

While school violence itself is not new, the issues surrounding school violence have become serious problems for American schools and universities. The tragic events at Columbine caused a renewed public outcry over issues of school safety and violence prevention, raising new questions about how educators should prepare for the unpredictable, unimaginable possibility of violence at school. Many schools are struggling to balance the need for security with the need for quality education; the two needs often compete for the same resources in a time of rising costs and shrinking budgets. Meanwhile, schools also face challenging new government requirements for tracking and reporting both student performance and school safety.

Tracking School Violence

One of the biggest challenges facing educators today is to accurately assess and study the scope of school violence in America. But because no national standard reporting system strictly identifies what is meant by school violence, measuring how much violence occurs in schools can be difficult. Individual schools are left to determine what school violence is, and the scope of incident reporting is voluntary. Some schools report only incidents involving guns or other weapons, while others also count physical fights and bullying as violent acts. This produces mixed results that may not always reflect the scope of school violence.

Some statistics show that school violence has increased by as much as 10 percent since 1999, including the incidents of school violence that actually occurred as well as the number of plots that were stopped before they could be carried out. The U.S. Centers for Disease Control and Prevention reports that youth violence is the second leading cause of death for young people between the ages of ten and twenty-four. Other reports show that incidents of school violence have decreased by half since 1992, and the American Bar Association has observed that a child is three times more likely to be struck by lightning than to be killed violently at school.

To add to the confusion, some experts say that the No Child Left Behind Act (NCLB), which became a national law in 2002, encour-

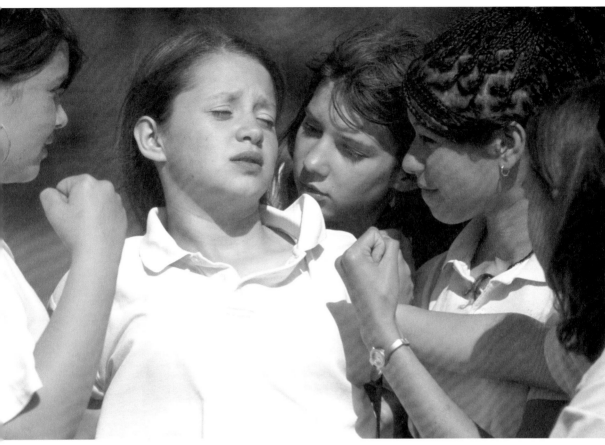

The experts have differing opinions about the rates of school violence in the nation's schools.

ages inaccurate reporting of school violence. NCLB was intended to improve American education by ensuring equality among all the schools in the country. NCLB requires all schools to use standard education methods and regular testing to prove that students are able to achieve certain goals at each grade level. The law also requires schools to maintain a safe atmosphere for learning. Schools that fail to meet these requirements may lose a portion of their government funding. Because most public schools in the United States rely on money from the government to stay open, NCLB provides a powerful incentive to meet these requirements. Many parents, educators, and advocacy groups therefore believe that NCLB is an incentive to underreport school violence.

School Responses

Uncertainty about the prevalence of school violence has caused parents in many communities throughout the country to demand more security measures at schools. Schools have responded by hiring more security guards, installing metal detectors and security cameras, and implementing dress codes and zero tolerance policies. Some schools conduct emergency evacuation drills and control access to school buildings by locking certain doors during specific times of the day. These restrictions and prevention methods are sometimes supplemented by student programs in conflict resolution, youth leadership, mentoring, parent involvement, and training in unarmed self-defense for students and teachers. But despite the best efforts of school administrators and security professionals, school violence still occurs. Although no ideal solution has yet been found, educators continue to work in partnership with parents, students, and communities to prevent school violence in the future.

Examining School Violence

In *Issues That Concern You: School Violence*, the authors debate these and other aspects of the school violence problem in excerpts from articles, books, reports, and other sources. In addition, the volume also includes resources for further investigation. The "Organizations to Contact" section directs students to organizations that are working on issues surrounding school violence. The bibliography highlights recent books and periodicals for more in-depth study, while the appendix "What You Should Know About School Violence" outlines basic facts and statistics, and "What You Should Do About School Violence" helps students use their knowledge to help themselves and others. Taken together, these features make *Issues That Concern You: School Violence* a valuable resource for anyone researching this issue.

ONE

School Violence Is Increasing

Adrienne Mand Lewin

> Adrienne Mand Lewin is an independent journalist who
> has contributed to ABC News, FOXNews.com, and Word
> Smitten.com. In the following viewpoint Lewin presents
> the argument that school-related violence is on the rise.
> Lewin observes that the number of incidents of school vio-
> lence has increased since the Columbine High School
> shootings in 1999. She examines the underlying causes of
> this increase and discusses school violence prevention
> efforts. Although school security programs have improved,
> schools still need to make the problem of increasing school
> violence a priority.

With two foiled school shootings in the past week [in late
April 2006], the question remains whether students are
any safer than they were before the violence at Columbine High
School that left 13 dead and 25 injured [in 1999].

Those who work with schools to prevent violence say they get
high marks for increasing awareness and reporting threats, but
they note that schools face budget and time cuts that could make
further safeguarding difficult.

"The best news is that there has been a change since Columbine
by adults working with kids to change the mind-set that reporting

Adrienne Mand Lewin, "Are Schools Safer Post-Columbine?" ABC News, April 24, 2006.
Reproduced by permission.

incidents is not snitching," said Kenneth Trump, president of National School Safety and Security Services, a school safety consulting firm. "It could be saving somebody's life, including their own. More and more students are coming forward," he said.

An Increase in Violence

At the same time, Trump's organization has tracked 10 thwarted school violence plots since March 1 of this year [2006], as well as 78 nonfatal school-related shootings, up from 52 during the entire 2004–05 school year and 68 in the 2003–04 school year.

"Even though we tend to see more incidents at this time of year [spring], the spate of incidents since March 1 [2006] seems to be a lot," Trump said. "The good news is schools and law enforcement partner agencies are doing a better job at preventing these incidents. Any one of these incidents could have been the next Columbine if students hadn't reported [threats] and adults hadn't responded."

Two of those incidents include a middle school in North Pole, Alaska, where six students were arrested and nine others suspended for allegedly plotting to kill students and teachers with guns and knives. And another plot, in which five teens in Kansas were arrested for allegedly planning to shoot up their school on the Columbine anniversary, April 20, before details were discovered on the Web site MySpace.com.

"The only thing that really scares me more than kids with a plot to cause harm to a school are adults who believe it couldn't happen here," he said. "Nobody wants to be alarmist . . . but we've seen an uptick in school-associated violence over the past three years [2003–2006]."

Less Money for School Security

Jane Grady, assistant director of the Center for the Study and Prevention of Violence at the University of Colorado at Boulder, said violence prevention got a lot of attention from school administrators and program funding from federal, state and local governments following Columbine.

"When things happen, right after Columbine, there was a lot of money for schools," Grady said. "As we move further away . . . even

Teachers and administrators at the Cicely Tyson School of Performing and Fine Arts in New Jersey have developed a program, Teens Against Violence Everywhere, in an effort to keep teens out of harm's way.

some foundations, their priorities shift. That's just the way it is. Other things float to the top."

Some of the funding for such programs comes from the Department of Education's Office of Safe and Drug-Free Schools, which lost $100 million in congressional funding this year [2006], said Bill Modzeleski, associate assistant deputy secretary for the office.

The state grants program was deemed ineffective and funds were being distributed too thinly, with about 60 percent of school districts receiving less than $10,000, he said. The cut money was put into a competitive discretionary grant program. The president's budget calls for the entire $330 million program to be cut in 2007.

Trump said the funding issue isn't just about broad-based security systems placed in schools but "anything from two-way radios to staff training."

More Emphasis on Standardized Tests Instead of Security

At the same time, Grady said, school administrators say schools are dedicating more time to meeting mandated testing standards, which cuts into time for programs such as violence prevention.

"There has been a lot of movement to trying to make schools safer. People are certainly aware of what's going on out there," Grady said, adding, "They're more concerned now with bringing up their test scores. That's where a lot of the focus seems to be right now."

Trump said his group's research supports that notion. "There's an enormous amount of pressure on school administrators to meet standards," he said. "It's not political, it's an administrative thing. Anything that's not direct instructional time is falling to the back burner."

Ronald Stephens, executive director of the nonprofit National School Safety Center, said one example of the shifting focus is that the federal government provided funding for more than 6,000 school safety resource officers with the expectation that state and local agencies would continue to pay for the program when the federal program ended.

"The reality is that funding goes away," Stephens said, adding, "Clearly, there's a function of what are the priorities at the school, but if you want to meet the test scores it's critically important to have a safe and welcoming environment."

School Security and Violence Prevention

According to a 2002 study by the Secret Service National Threat Assessment Center and the Safe and Drug-Free Schools Program, which identified 37 incidents involving 41 school attacks that had

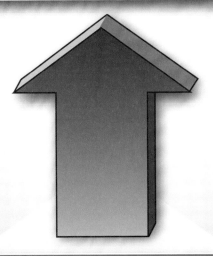

Violence Is on the Rise

In the 2003–2004 school year, 81 percent of schools reported one or more violent incidents.

In the 1999–2000 school year, 71 percent of schools reported one or more violent incidents.

Taken from: *Indicators of School Crime and Safety: 2006*, U.S. Departments of Education and Justice, 2006.

occurred between 1974 and 2000, most attackers display pre-attack behavior that can signal a potential for violence. At that time, the study said, some 80 percent of school shooters spoke about their plans to other students, but their peers rarely told adults.

"They're not impulsive—there's planning involved," Modzeleski said. There also was access to weapons and bullying was a factor in about two-thirds of the cases, according to the report. "More and more these kids are communicating with each other via the Internet," he said, as was the case in Kansas. "I think that both schools did the right thing in also getting law enforcement involved right away."

Tracking and Preventing School Violence

It is difficult to fully tally school violence incidents because there is no federally mandated tracking, Trump said, but anecdotally, reports are increasing.

"Outside of the shootings, we're hearing consistently from the school administrators and schools across the country that aggressive behavior and school violence-related safety issues are on the upswing," he said. "Federal statistics tend to understate; public perception tends to overstate. The actual number exists somewhere in between—we don't know where exactly."

In some communities, the violence can be attributed to gangs, he said, but there is another consistent factor: human complacency. "I think that school officials are concerned about safety," he said. "I think it's just a matter of fighting obstacles—funding, time, denial in their own school communities."

Making Schools Safer

At the same time, Stephens said, schools have greatly improved their work with law enforcement and students to stop attacks before they occur. "The real issue is more of a mind-set that's established on campus, a spirit and a message that threats will not be tolerated," he said. "They will be taken seriously. They will follow up on these, and there is a point where a threat goes from an idle manner to a criminal offense."

Modzeleski said much of what can be done to prevent violence doesn't require "big-ticket items." "Monitoring your students, knowing who your students are," he said. "We think it's essential that kids are connected to an adult in a school . . . because most of the kids we interviewed as part of our study felt there was nobody in school they could go to."

TWO

School Violence Is Decreasing

John Stossel

John Stossel is a correspondent for ABC News and coanchor of the television news program *20/20*. In the following viewpoint Stossel argues that U.S. public schools are safe and that violence in schools is decreasing. Stossel presents the idea that constant news coverage of rare school shootings makes people believe that schools are more violent than they actually are. Public fears about widespread school violence are not supported by reported statistics about the occurrence of violence in schools, according to Stossel. He concludes that children are safer in schools than they are in almost any other place.

The randomness of the Virginia Tech shootings, and the way we hear the gory, horrific details reported over and over can make us lose perspective. One psychologist issued a press release saying, "We need to take action now to . . . end this epidemic of violence."

California legislators held special hearings on campus safety, and Sen. Dianne Feinstein, D-Calif., said she hoped this would "reignite the dormant effort to pass common-sense gun regulations in this nation." Please. That's a lot of reaction for something that almost never happens.

John Stossel, "The School Violence Myth," ABC News, April 17, 2007. Reproduced by permission.

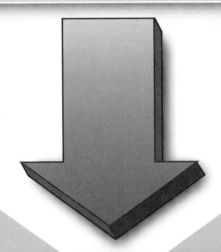

Violence Is Decreasing

In 1992, there were 140 violent incidents in public schools per 1,000 students.

In 2004, there were 48 violent incidents in public schools per 1,000 students.

Taken from: *Indicators of School Crime and Safety: 2006*, U.S. Departments of Education and Justice, 2006.

School Violence Is a Myth

Many Americans believe schools are more dangerous than ever, but that's a myth! It's one of many I've discovered in 36 years of consumer reporting.

In the early '90s—the first years records were kept—there were more than 40 deaths just from K–12 school shootings per year. Since then, the death toll has been trending down, not up.

MYTH: Schools are violent.

TRUTH: Schools are pretty safe.

Media bad news bears love crime and violence. Terrible things are happening, and everyone knows they're happening much more often. The gory pictures and the excited copy conceal the actual truth: America is safer than almost any country in human history.

The Virginia Tech shooting has resurrected the fears that the Columbine, Jonesboro and Paducah school shootings created during the late 1990s. Those killings triggered a regular spate of sto-

Some experts say that media sensationalism about school violence causes schools to spend money on security measures, such as armed guards, that are not needed.

ries about "spreading school violence." But school violence in America had been steadily decreasing. Violent crimes in schools dropped by half between 1992 and 2002, although reporting about school violence increased.

The shooting incidents are awful but aberrant; more Americans die from lightning strikes than from school violence. More kids die in bathtubs. But the media had become obsessed with school violence. After Columbine, my network aired 383 stories about the tragedy. Sam Donaldson warned wary parents and students about "angry teens turning up in other towns." CBS News correspondent Bob McNamara called school shootings "an American nightmare that too many schools know too well."

Students Are Safe at School

But it wasn't a nightmare that schools knew well. In fact, students are probably safer in school than they are at home or at the mall. Crime statistics show that kids are twice as likely to be victims of violence away from school than they are in school.

The media hysteria encouraged people who run schools to do crazy things, like spend thousands of dollars on security cameras, and hire police officers to guard the doors. Some schools terrified students by running SWAT team drills; cops burst into classrooms and ordered kids down to the floor. The result? Students felt less secure than ever before. Though school violence was down, studies show kids were more scared. "They can't learn under these conditions," said psychologist Frank Farley, former head of the American Psychological Association.

To listen to the media, Farley told me, you'd have to believe that Chicken Little was right. "The sky is truly falling. America is in terrible straits and our schools are a mess and they're violent. But they are not violent. I don't know why there is all this press coverage, other than the need for a story," said Farley.

That's it. The media beast must be fed. Scares drive up ratings.

THREE

No Child Left Behind Act Discourages Accurate Reporting of School Violence

Lisa Snell

Lisa Snell is the director of education and child welfare at Reason Foundation. She is also a frequent contributor to publications including *USA Today*, *School Reform News*, and *Privatization Watch*. In the following viewpoint Snell argues that schools are not accurately reporting the number and frequency of violent incidents. This circumstance has resulted in almost all public schools being labeled as safe, when in fact some schools are persistently dangerous. Snell states that the reporting requirements of the No Child Left Behind Act encourage schools to underreport incidents of violence in order to avoid being labeled as dangerous. Snell discusses the differences in defining and reporting school violence across the country and gives examples of better reporting methods.

The federal No Child Left Behind Act [NCLB] requires students in violent or dangerous schools to be given the option to transfer to safer schools. Yet we find that school districts across the nation have manipulated safety criteria to their advantage, resulting in nearly every public school being labeled as safe—irrespective of the actual dangers to children at the school.

The Unsafe School Choice Option (USCO) (section 9532 of the Elementary and Secondary Education Act [ESEA] of 1965, as amended by the No Child Left Behind Act of 2001) requires that each state receiving funds under the ESEA establishes and implements a statewide policy requiring that students attending a persistently dangerous public elementary or secondary school, or students who become victims of a violent criminal offense while in or on the grounds of a public school that they attend, be allowed to attend a safe public school.

School Violence Is Underreported

In the 2003–2004 school year only about 50 of the nation's 92,000 public schools were labeled "persistently dangerous" under the No Child Left Behind Act. Based on the small number of schools that were labeled as dangerous, in September 2003, the Education Reform Subcommittee held a field hearing in Denver, Colorado, to study how states are implementing No Child Left Behind's persistently dangerous schools provision. The hearing suggested some states are significantly underreporting the number of unsafe schools to sidestep the law's requirements. Testimony from a National Center for Education Statistics expert revealed that in 2001, 6 percent of students reported they had carried a weapon on school property, and the same percentage feared being attacked at school. A year earlier, in 2000, students were victims of about 700,000 nonfatal violent crimes while on school property. However, only 0.0006 percent of the nation's schools have been designated as "unsafe" by their states.

Similarly, in a 2003 survey of school-based police officers with 728 respondents, representing each of the 50 United States, over 87 percent of these police officers reported that the numbers of crimes that occur on school campuses nationwide are underreported to police. In addition, over 61 percent of survey respondents believe that school administrators faced with their schools possibly being labeled as "persistently dangerous" will underreport school crime.

Identifying Dangerous Schools

Most of the problem with the underreporting of dangerous schools comes from the state definitions of "persistently dangerous." The NCLB federal law allows each state to use its own definition of persistently dangerous. The majority of states have set such a high threshold of violence that it is unlikely that *any* schools will be labeled as dangerous.

In response to states refusing to identify dangerous schools, the U.S. Department of Education issued new non-regulatory guidelines for the unsafe school choice component of NCLB. In the new guidance the Education Department encouraged states to use a shorter time period to evaluate a dangerous school and to eval-

The No Child Left Behind Act has been critized for uneven guidelines on reporting school violence incidents.

uate all incidents of school violence. Currently, the majority of state definitions requires schools to be dangerous for three years before being labeled as "persistently dangerous" and often only include gun violations as part of the definition. More specifically the guidelines state:

> Often-identified measures of danger include number of weapons seized, number of assaults reported by students, and number of homicides. We strongly encourage SEAs (state education associations) to work with local law enforcement officials, including school resource officers, to identify other sources of data and information that can be used to accurately assess whether a school is persistently dangerous. Many current State definitions utilize suspension and expulsion data, which measure disciplinary responses to an incident. We urge SEAs to use data that relate to incidents (numbers of offenses) even when an offender is not apprehended and subsequently disciplined.

Failing to Identify Dangerous Schools

Clearly, these new guidelines are designed to encourage states to take an honest look at school violence in their schools. Yet, despite the new guidelines the 2004 school year seems to be following the trend of few states truthfully labeling dangerous schools. For example, in 2004 not a single school in New York State is "persistently dangerous," according to the State Education Department. California has also found no dangerous schools in 2004.

Newspapers around the nation are filled with horror stories of school violence that was not considered in a state's definition of dangerous schools. In Georgia, which had no dangerous schools in 2004, an investigation by the *Atlanta Journal-Constitution* found thousands of crimes that were not being considered by the state as it compiled its list of dangerous schools. Marietta City Schools did not report an alleged rape, despite the fact that security cameras captured what school officials believed to be a 17-year-old male forcing a 16-year-old girl into the boys' restroom for sex. In Cherokee County, a pair of aggravated batteries that left one student with a broken jaw and another with facial fractures were not reported to the state because administrators did not list the infractions under aggravated batteries.

Similarly New York City has received negative press for failing to label schools as dangerous. New York defines a school as "persistently dangerous" if the number of incidents of weapons possession or use equals or exceeds 3 percent of the school's enrollment for two consecutive years, officials said. Officials said the finding was based on a decline in incidents involving weapons, but they said they did not include factors like assault, sexual assault and other violent incidents, citing significant inconsistencies in the data reported by schools.

According to the [New York] *Daily News*, these incidents were among those not counted as dangerous by the Education Department:

- Three male students at Intermediate School 172 in Harlem forced a girl into a closet and sexually assaulted her in March.

- A student at Manhattan's Washington Irving High School shoved a Snapple machine down a flight of stairs in December.

- A student at Queens' Beach Channel High School in December smashed his ex-girlfriend's head through a trophy case.

Problems with Reporting Violence

Most state definitions of dangerous schools continue to go against recent recommendations on dangerous schools established by the U.S. Department of Education. In a September 2004 report the Education Commission of the States (ECS) cataloged the 50 state definitions for persistently dangerous schools. The ECS analysis found that the majority of states still use three years as the time period that a school must be dangerous before being labeled and fewer than 10 states have adopted the federal recommendation for considering crimes over a one-year period. In addition, many states continue to use a narrow definition of incidents that considers gun violations as the main criteria for a dangerous school. For example, in California a school is only dangerous if for three consecutive years it has a federal or state gun-free schools violation or a violent criminal offense has been committed by a student or a non-student on school property *and* has one expulsion for every 100 enrolled students for a serious violent offense.

Some states have thresholds of school violence ensuring that no schools will ever be labeled. For example, in Colorado for a school over 1200 students, it must have more than 225 violent incidents for 1200 students for two consecutive years. In other words, a violent high school in Colorado would have to have a violent incident *every* school day for two years.

Regardless of official lists of persistently dangerous schools, some school leaders have maintained their own list of dangerous schools and given these schools extra resources and attention. For example, Philadelphia Public School CEO Paul Vallas told the *Philadelphia*

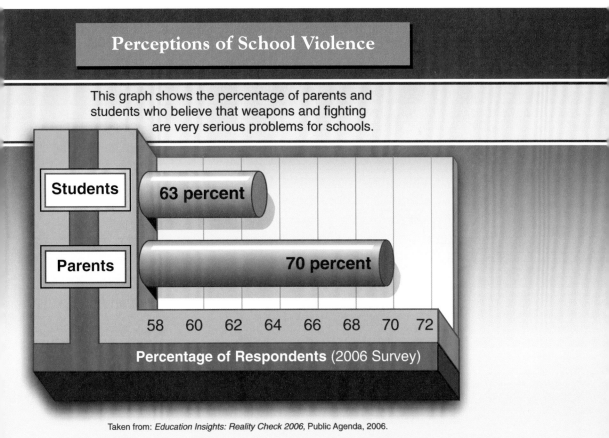

Perceptions of School Violence

This graph shows the percentage of parents and students who believe that weapons and fighting are very serious problems for schools.

Students — 63 percent

Parents — 70 percent

58   60   62   64   66   68   70   72

Percentage of Respondents (2006 Survey)

Taken from: *Education Insights: Reality Check 2006*, Public Agenda, 2006.

Daily News that despite the state's list, he has his own list of 50 disruptive schools that will get extra behavioral health staffers and security measures. "The state has its list, and I have my list. My list is larger than the state's," Vallas said. Similarly, in New York City the [Mayor Michael] Bloomberg administration has targeted several dangerous schools with extra resources that have not been labeled as "persistently dangerous" by the state.

School districts have also had problems with data collection. Washington D.C. has become the poster child for how *not* to collect school violence data.

In September 2004 the *Washington Post* reported that the District's school system does not keep adequate records on crimes and other serious incidents that occur on school grounds, according to an audit by D.C.'s inspector general. An audit by the inspector general's office concluded that the schools lack a comprehensive system to record and track incidents from the time they occur to the completion of investigations by police and school security officers. In addition, the reporting of serious incidents is hampered by school security policies that are inconsistent or unclear. The auditors found that "there is no central repository, automated or manual" within the school system to keep track of the final outcome of incidents.

Reported Information Is Too Old

In addition to problems with data collection, school violence reporting also suffers from schools being labeled based on old data. There is a huge lag in data reporting. For example, in Reason's analysis of school district reporting of crime data, the school districts that made any information available at all often reported data that were from two to five years old.

School violence crime data in New York City provides a good example of why good data collection is critical. The most dangerous high schools identified by the New York Police Department in 2004, based on the actual number of violent incidents that occurred in the schools, were not the same schools that the education department had identified as dangerous schools in need of extra resources. In other words, the New York Department of Education had been providing extra resources and police officers for schools that were dangerous but were not the *most* dangerous schools according to the actual data.

A Better Reporting System

Pennsylvania has created a statewide school violence incident reporting system that should solve both the timeliness issue and the inconsistent data reporting by school districts within a state. According to a May 2004 *Philadelphia Inquirer* article, a partnership between the Pennsylvania Department of Education and the state's 501 school districts has resulted in a much-improved online system for tracking violent incidents in Pennsylvania schools. "This system will not only allow the Commonwealth to meet the requirements of the federal No Child Left Behind Act but will give parents a precise picture of their child's school environment," said [Pennsylvania] Secretary [of Education, Vicki] Phillips. "We are taking advantage of the best that high-tech collaboration can provide. The online reporting system gives school district administrators explicit definitions of what incidents should or should not be included in the annual report." Florida also has a statewide data reporting system that is easily accessible to parents and is the only state where crime data is presented alongside academic data to give parents a clearer picture of a school's performance and environment.

State legislators should follow Florida and Pennsylvania's example and create standard statewide reporting systems that are automated and take advantage of on-line technology. Legislators should also make crime statistics available as a standard feature of school report cards.

FOUR

School Violence Can Be Prevented

Don Fraser

> Don Fraser is a veteran law enforcement officer and pub-
> lic safety specialist. In the following viewpoint Fraser
> argues that school violence can be prevented. He discuss-
> es various ways in which schools can better protect stu-
> dents and teachers from potential violence. Fraser states
> that schools are safer when educators work with parents
> and students to raise awareness of school violence and
> prevention. Examples of successful prevention strategies
> are included.

Violence has shaken many schools across the country. More
than two dozen school shootings have occurred since the
[2006–2007] school year began; yet there is hope. Communities
are banding together to protect their children. Schools are working on many fronts to curb aggression and keep students out of
harm's way.

There is no magic answer to keeping violence out of schools.
It requires a multifaceted effort from administrators, staff, parents
and students. Available strategies include peer mediation and conflict resolution training, video analytics in school "hot spots," and
teaching students how to use the Internet safely.

Don Fraser, "Proactive Prevention," *American School and University*, February 1, 2007. Reproduced
by permission.

Teaching Conflict Resolution

Numerous methods are available for defusing conflicts before they erupt. Teaching conflict-resolution techniques to students and teachers can give them the skills to resolve disagreements, deal with bullies, and cope with other issues that can spin out of control if not addressed quickly. Schools should teach students ways to "cool down" when angered. Many schools also are training staff members and students as conflict mediators. If a quarrel is escalating, those involved could be brought before a peer counselor as an alternative form of discipline.

The National Crime Prevention Council also has developed programs that help students become part of the solution to school violence. Likewise, Project Citizen's "We the People" program teaches students constitutional responsibility, engaging them in

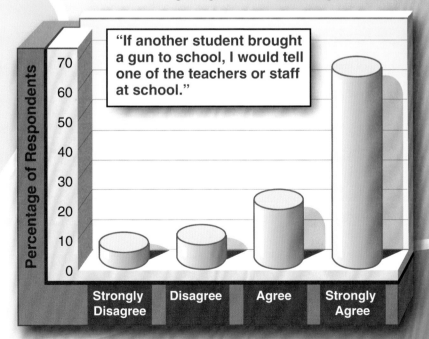

Students Are Willing to Play a Role in Preventing Violence Among Their Peers

This chart shows the responses 9th grade students in Virginia gave to the following statement:

"If another student brought a gun to school, I would tell one of the teachers or staff at school."

Taken from: *Virginia High School Safety Study,* University of Virginia, 2008.

shaping long-term fixes within their own school. The program helps young people learn how to influence public policy. In the process, they develop support for democratic values and principles, tolerance and feelings of political efficacy. Ultimately, the younger we can reach children and give them tools for resolving conflicts, the greater success we will have in preventing violence.

Safety Online

One critical area that needs attention is students' Internet use. Countless young people share photos and other personal information on social networking sites such as MySpace. Sites such as these say they restrict children under 18 from posting, but there's little monitoring to enforce this rule. Many kids don't think twice about putting addresses, ages, schools they attend and photos on their Web pages. They may not realize that anyone with Internet access, including sexual predators, can use that information to track them down. Even seemingly innocuous information such as the type of music and movies a child likes may give predators enough information to wile their way into a child's life. An online predator can pretend to be another kid, sharing the same likes and dislikes. He or she can establish a rapport with a child and soon may suggest a face-to-face meeting.

This problem has become so pervasive that some school officials have taken disciplinary action against underage students who have created pages on MySpace or other social networking sites.

There is another strong incentive to refrain from using these sites. Some colleges search social networking sites to learn whether prospective students are engaging in unsafe online behavior. Parents and teachers need to educate students about the ramifications involved with disclosing information on the Internet and the dangers of meeting new friends online. In many states, the attorney general's office has set up branches to help parents teach children safe Internet skills.

The rules for using the Internet that parents and administrators should impose on children are simple: Don't let them agree to meet someone that they have met online. Don't let them share identifying information such as a name, address, phone number, age or school name. Prohibit them from using a chat room without supervision. Tell them not to open e-mails from people they don't know and to make sure they tell an adult if something online makes them uncomfortable or suspicious.

School Security Cameras

About 70 percent of the nation's schools do not use security cameras. These devices can be an integral component for protecting public safety; they can deter illicit activities, create a visual record of incidents and provide an early warning of potential hazards. The state of Washington recently enacted a mandate to place surveillance cameras in all middle schools. Schools considering surveillance systems should first notify parents of their intentions so there is clear communication about the goals. The best approach is to install cameras in areas that are common violence "hot spots"—gyms, cafeterias, hallways and outside school buildings.

Although a majority of U.S. schools do not use security cameras, this kind of surveillance system can be a key component in efforts to reduce school violence.

Video surveillance technology can alert security personnel of potential safety concerns. Cameras can be programmed to identify suspicious activity and alert authorities immediately. For example, if a system detects someone loitering on school grounds, a signal can be sent to a security officer, who can take control of the surveillance camera to investigate further. The security system also can be used to establish a perimeter around the campus so that authorities are notified instantly if someone enters the premises during the school day. Instead of relying exclusively on security personnel to catch suspicious activity, video systems provide a consistent means to identify and thwart threats.

Many schools have their surveillance systems tied to the local police department so that when suspicious activity occurs, police can monitor what is occurring. In a scenario in which hostages are involved, video could be critical to their safety, as well as to the safety of an entry team planning an approach. The visual footage gives officers a better sense of what is going to happen when they walk into a school under siege. Schools also can share floor plans and architectural features of the school building so that in an emergency, first responders can lay out a tactical plan before they arrive on the scene.

Better Communication

Many school administrators have conducted risk assessments to identify potential vulnerabilities, such as access points to a facility. Entranceways should be monitored regularly.

In a high-stress situation, it is easy for communications to break down. Some parents may be frantic, and school officials won't have the resources to call parents individually. Cell phone systems are inadequate in many crises—it took just 15 minutes for cell circuits in Pearl, Miss., to become saturated after a school shooting incident there.

New emergency communication alert systems provide automatic alerts so that everyone—from crisis teams to parents to the media—is kept informed at the touch of a button. School administrators should clearly explain the communication policies to parents ahead of time so they know what to expect.

Involving Parents

Technology alone will not stem the tide of violence in schools. The more parents are involved in their children's lives and their school communities, the less likely their children are to behave violently in school. Schools should encourage parents to watch whom their children are spending time with in and out of school. Foster an environment where parents can communicate regularly with one another to share concerns.

Parents and teachers should pay attention to changes in a child's behavior. Warning signs may include a child's developing an obsession with violence or weapons, experiencing a significant drop in grades, or avoiding school and other activities. Unexplained bruises or a need for extra money could indicate that a child is a victim of bullying.

The first response in the wake of school shootings has been to reassure parents, yet it is equally important to be upfront with students so they will feel safe. Teachers should have honest discussions with students. Address the questions they will be asking themselves: What if it happens here? Create a forum where students can voice their fears and concerns. Also, give students a mechanism to share tips or report suspicious activity anonymously.

FIVE

School Violence Cannot Be Prevented

Associated Press

The following viewpoint argues that school violence cannot be anticipated or prevented. Incidents of violence at schools are too unpredictable to prevent, and schools should focus instead on preparing to react safely. Schools can best protect students by having emergency response plans in place. Students and teachers should be trained to respond quickly and safely to an emergency or violent incident.

A gunman kills several students in a one-room Amish schoolhouse in Pennsylvania. In Colorado, a drifter walks into a school and fatally shoots a student before taking his own life. Wisconsin authorities charge three boys with plotting a bomb attack on their high school and, two weeks later, a student in a rural school allegedly shoots his principal. A gunman bursts into a Vermont elementary school looking for his ex-girlfriend and guns down a teacher.

All of this in [September 2006] alone.

Can School Violence Be Stopped?

Since the 1999 Columbine massacre that left 15 people dead, there has been a determined effort among administrators, principals and teachers to improve school safety. Law enforcement officers across the nation and around the world have added training specifically intended to address school violence.

But experts say there is simply no way to guarantee that a stranger or student won't be able to injure or kill on school grounds. "There's no perfect security, from the White House to the schoolhouse," said Kenneth Trump, president of the National School Safety and Security Services consulting firm in Cleveland.

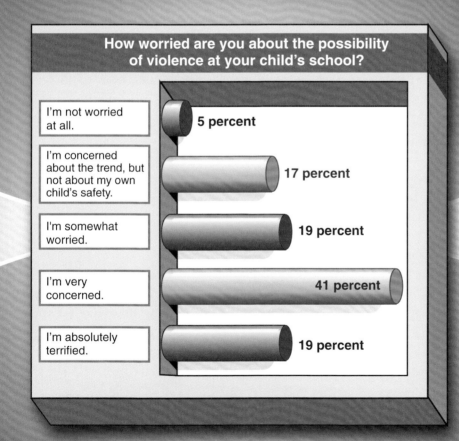

Most Parents Are Concerned About School Safety

How worried are you about the possibility of violence at your child's school?

Response	Percent
I'm not worried at all.	5 percent
I'm concerned about the trend, but not about my own child's safety.	17 percent
I'm somewhat worried.	19 percent
I'm very concerned.	41 percent
I'm absolutely terrified.	19 percent

Taken from: School Violence Poll, ParentCenter.com.

Violence Is Unpredictable

Since Columbine, school officials have gotten better at preventing student violence, he said, but authorities can't prepare for every problem. "When you factor in unpredictable outsiders, when you have a roaming monster walking into the schools, we have to be realistic," Trump said. "There are some incidents you're not going to be able to prevent."

Trump's firm counts 17 nonfatal school shootings so far this school year [2006–2007] beginning Aug. 1. There were 85 the previous school year and 52 in the 2004–2005 school year.

Since Columbine in 1999, the number of fatal school shootings in a school year has ranged from three (2002–03) to 24 (2004–05), according to National School Safety and Security Services. The firm does not track cases before Columbine.

Park County Sheriff Fred Wegener was among the law enforcement officials who eagerly applied for federal aid to beef up security at Platte Canyon High School in Bailey [Colorado], the site of [a September 2006] attack in which a man held six girls hostage before killing one and himself.

A deputy was assigned to be the school's resource officer—essentially, its security guard. But that guard was called away on sheriff's business and gunman Duane Morrison walked inside with two handguns. He reportedly sat in the school parking lot and wandered the hallways for as long as 35 minutes before the siege began.

Responding to Violence

Despite the death of 16-year-old Emily Keyes, things could have been worse, authorities said. "Basically, the tragedy of Columbine taught law enforcement and educators how to avoid future tragedies," Gov. Bill Owens said. "In a couple of significant ways, the tragedy of Columbine may have helped prevent an even worse tragedy (here)."

He said educators had been instructed in August on what to do. The school was also designed using concepts learned from the Columbine attacks, which helped authorities keep the gunman in one room.

Preparing for the Unpredictable

Ever since Columbine, school officials have been taught to write emergency response plans and practice them, to lock down schools and evacuate when it appears safe. That seemed to work well in Bailey as hundreds of students were whisked to safety.

Law enforcement officers who once were taught to set up a perimeter and wait for SWAT teams to show up are now trained in "active shooter" programs that call for the first officers on the scene to enter the building and work as quickly as possible to locate the gunman, Trump said.

"That's why we were able to isolate it to just one room and get everybody else out," Wegener said. "Still, you can't prepare for something like this. You do the best you can."

Student Zach Barnes, 16, also said students practiced drills for emergencies including a gunman in the school. Students were told to remain calm, taught where to go and how to leave the

Some experts say that school violence is unavoidable and that having emergency responders and students participate in disaster drills is critical.

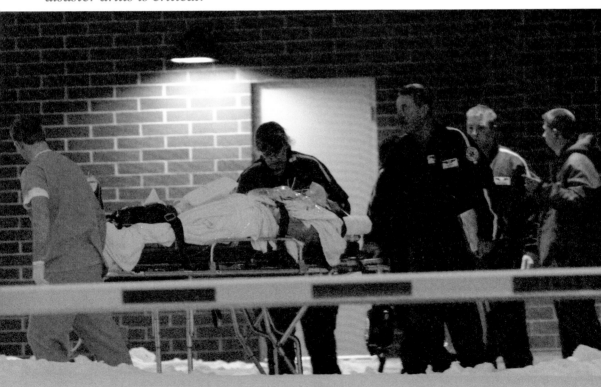

school. Still, there appeared to be at least one glitch [in the Bailey incident].

"We were sitting there in math class and over the intercom they said, 'Students and teachers, we have a code white, repeat code white,' and nobody really knew what a code white was," Barnes said.

He said his teacher pulled a sheet of paper from her desk, checked it and then herded her students into a nearby classroom that had a solid door. After about 25 minutes, a police officer led them into the hallway and out of the school.

Improving School Security

Colorado has left decisions on providing security in schools up to some 172 school boards, but state lawmakers said they will look at training and other issues following the Bailey attack.

Providing security guards at every entrance to every school would be difficult, said Senate President Joan Fitz-Gerald, D-Golden, but others said video cameras and security systems could help fill the gap.

"If we could plug in some technology, that would help," said George Voorheis, superintendent of Colorado's largely rural Montrose & Olathe Schools District RE1J.

SIX

Guns Increase the Risk of School Violence

Judith Kafka

> Judith Kafka is an assistant professor at Baruch College in New York City whose research focuses on education reform. In the following viewpoint Kafka argues that easy access to guns is the main cause of violence in schools. Kafka discusses several school shooting incidents and identifies the similarities and differences in each case. Kafka states that availability of guns was a common factor in all cases. She cites a lack of adequate gun control as one of the primary reasons for continuing violence in schools.

In the spring of 1999, when two male students went on a shooting rampage at Columbine High School in Jefferson County, Colo., killing 13 others before turning the guns on themselves, it didn't take long for politicians, journalists, and advocates of small-school-centered reform to point to the large size of Columbine as a key factor in the tragedy. The sheer size of the facility, they argued, and the fact that the school enrolled close to 2,000 students, created an alienating environment, one in which troubled youths like the two shooters were allowed to drift unknown, becoming increasingly angry and isolated.

Hillary Clinton, while campaigning for the U.S. Senate in New York, noted that the principal of Columbine High School had

Judith Kafka, "It's Guns, Not School Size," *Education Week*, December 26, 2007. Copyright © 2007 Editorial Projects in Education. Reproduced by permission of the author.

never heard of the "trench coat mafia," a group to which the two students responsible for the shootings were said to have belonged, and faulted the school's size in part for what had occurred there. Educational researchers and activists who supported small-school reform made similar claims—often in the pages of *Education Week*. They ominously warned that shootings were likely to happen in other large schools where students lacked a sense of community and belonging. Their words seemed prophetic when, nearly two years later, a male student at a large high school in suburban Southern California opened fire, killing two and injuring 13.

By then, the specter of Columbine had been used to promote small-school reform nationwide. The [Bill] Clinton administration cited the need to prevent similar tragedies as it set aside $120 million for a "Small, Safe, and Successful High Schools" initiative in 2000. An oft-cited report on small-school reform in Chicago referred to Columbine as a "reminder" of what could happen in large schools in which students and teachers failed to form strong relationships. Advocates of small schools have continued to blame the large, "factory model" high school for school shootings in the years since, arguing that acts of gun violence are unlikely to occur in small schools—where everyone is known, students have a sense of belonging, and personal relationships exist between young people and caring adults.

School Size Is Not a Factor

Yet as the school shooting this past October at SuccessTech, a 250-student school in Cleveland, demonstrated, blaming the size of schools for acts of gun violence is at best naive, and at worst opportunistic and disingenuous. There may be other good reasons for reconfiguring large urban high schools into smaller ones, but preventing school shootings is not one of them.

The gun violence at SuccessTech, in which a 14-year-old boy shot and injured two students and two teachers before killing himself, was not the first such incident to occur in a small school. Westside Middle School, near Jonesboro, Ark., for example, enrolled only 250 students in 1998, when two boys shot and killed

Police respond to the SuccessTech shootings in Cleveland, Ohio. School shooting incidents like this one have been blamed on a lack of gun control laws.

four students and a teacher there and wounded many others. Heath High School in West Paducah, Ky., had an enrollment of around 550 when a 14-year-old boy opened fire at a group of students in 1997, killing three girls and wounding five others.

Unlike these other schools, however, SuccessTech is one of the many small schools of choice opened in urban districts across the country since Columbine—schools often promoted, at least in part, as a solution to school violence and student alienation. In fact, SuccessTech is precisely the kind of small school that reform advocates recommend. Funded in part by a grant from the Bill &

Melinda Gates Foundation, it is a highly selective school of choice, intentionally small, and has been successful by many measures—including a 94 percent graduation rate in a school system with an average rate of just 55 percent. Yet despite SuccessTech's smallness and selectivity, on Oct. 10, 2007, a boy came to school with a gun and opened fire.

Controlling Access to Guns

Predictably, in the days immediately following the shooting, questions were raised about what the school could have done to prevent it from occurring. Why hadn't more guards been assigned to SuccessTech? Why weren't students required to go through metal detectors as they entered school? Of course, one of the rationales for schools like SuccessTech is that such security measures are unnecessary in small settings where everyone is known and feels safe. And by most accounts students at SuccessTech were known, and did feel safe. Indeed, being known was not the problem for the shooter. He was known. But he was also troubled, regularly teased, and, most importantly, he had access to a gun.

In fact, what draws all the school shootings together, and what accounts for all of the gun violence in schools across the country, is that a troubled male youth had access to a gun. Certainly school leaders want to take whatever actions they can to prevent such horrors from occurring, but blaming the organizational structure or size of schools for acts of gun violence creates an expedient scapegoat and avoids targeting the real problem: guns themselves. Using tragedies like Columbine or SuccessTech to promote specific school reforms shifts attention away from the issue of gun control, and mutes what should be national outrage directed at those who oppose even the mildest measures intended to limit access to firearms.

Without guns, the shooters at Columbine and SuccessTech would still have been angry, even violent, boys, but they would not have been able to harm so many others so quickly—nor would they have been able to end their own lives so easily once they were done.

The Debate over Arming Teachers

An online public survey shows that most people do not want teachers to carry guns in school.

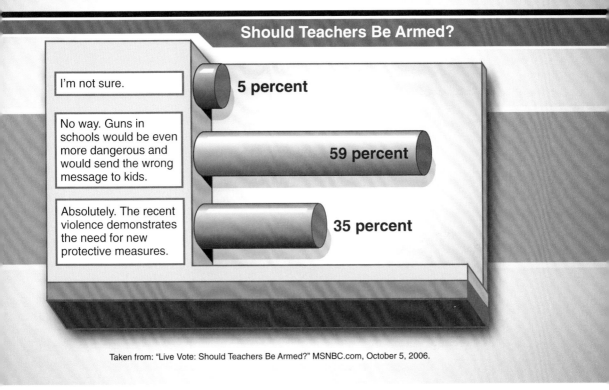

Should Teachers Be Armed?

I'm not sure.	5 percent
No way. Guns in schools would be even more dangerous and would send the wrong message to kids.	59 percent
Absolutely. The recent violence demonstrates the need for new protective measures.	35 percent

Taken from: "Live Vote: Should Teachers Be Armed?" MSNBC.com, October 5, 2006.

Other Factors in School Violence

There are other solutions to consider beyond gun control, of course. One would be to bar all troubled boys from school, and the increased focus on psychological profiling since the deadly shooting at Virginia Tech [in spring 2007] seems to point in this direction. Yet even if we could correctly identify all troubled young men, most do not open fire on their classmates and teachers, and they should be allowed to benefit from an education.

Another solution would be to eradicate all teasing and "bullying" in school, and in fact anti-bullying programs have become increasingly popular, and are even mandated in many districts—as are so-called "zero tolerance" discipline policies for bullying. But while they should never be condoned, teasing and bullying are somewhat nebulous acts. It is often difficult to distinguish the bully from the bullied, the students lashing out in self-defense from the instigators of the conflict. Nor is it clear that bullying itself is the cause of student alienation and malaise. We know that most youths who are bullied do not show up at school with a gun. Would the SuccessTech gunman not have opened fire on his classmates and teachers if he hadn't been teased in school? We don't know. We do know that he would not have been able to do so without a gun.

Blaming schools and school size for the gun violence that occurs within them is not only unfair and unreasonable, but it also distracts attention from the cause that those who care about school safety and youth violence should be fighting for: getting guns off our nation's streets and out of the hands of our nation's youths.

SEVEN

Guns Decrease the Risk of School Violence

Marshall Lewin

> Marshall Lewin is a frequent contributor to National Rifle Association (NRA) publications as well as the organization's Web site. In the following viewpoint Lewin argues that students and teachers should be allowed to carry concealed handguns on college campuses. Lewin states that many schools ban guns on campus even in states that allow citizens to carry guns in other public places. Students and teachers are left vulnerable and unprotected by the enforcement of gun-free school zones. Lewin argues that banning legal guns from schools will not stop criminals from bringing guns into schools but will prevent students and teachers from defending themselves in the event of violence. Lewin concludes that citizens have the right to self-defense and that right should extend to college campuses.

Should you have less freedom and safety than anyone else simply because you go to college?

Should society trust you less than your brothers and sisters of equal age simply because you attend college and they don't?

If you're mature enough and responsible enough to cast a vote, fight a war, own a gun, carry a gun and exercise every other right

Marshall Lewin, "The New Campus Revolt: Empty Holsters," National Rifle Association of America, Institute for Legislative Action, December 13, 2007. Reproduced by permission of the National Rifle Association.

of citizenship that every other adult citizen enjoys, then why should you be disarmed and defenseless at institutions of higher learning?

In the aftermath of last April's [2007] massacre at Virginia Tech, in which an armed maniac killed 27 students and five faculty members before killing himself, more and more students are asking life-and-death questions like these of their politicians and professors.

The Right to Self-Defense

It's a new national movement that's gathering momentum on college campuses across the country. In late October [2007] that movement took to the streets in the form of so-called "empty holster protests" at over 110 college campuses in 38 states and the District of Columbia. Led by a group called "Students for Concealed Carry on Campus," students wore empty holsters to protest state laws and student codes of conduct that prohibit them from exercising the Right to Carry on campus—even if they have Right-to-Carry permits.

"As a college student and a concealed handgun license holder, when I step onto campus I am left unable to defend myself," group founder Chris Brown, a political science major at North Texas University, says on the organization's website. "My state allows me to carry a handgun in public, but there is some imaginary line drawn around college campuses for silly reasons. And those silly reasons are getting people killed, raped and robbed."

Or, as one of the group's leaders notes in an e-mail signature evoking the tragedy at Virginia Tech, "Campus policies left students shooting back with camera phones. Life's worth more than pictures."

Yet many state legislatures and college administrators don't seem to think that students' lives—or the lives of faculty, staff and visitors—are worth as much as their own.

Bringing Guns to School

Even though 40 states have fair Right-to-Carry laws, 36 states ban carrying firearms at schools, while 20 of those specifically outlaw firearms on college campuses.

So far, only one state—Utah—specifically and expressly allows the Right to Carry on public college campuses, thanks to a 2004 law allowing the Right to Carry on all state property. Although the University of Utah challenged the law, the state Supreme Court upheld it.

Even before the shootings at Virginia Tech, many were calling for the Right to Carry to be restored on college campuses.

Students hold a candlelight vigil following the Virginia Tech shootings in 2007. Some argue that the shootings could possibly have been prevented had students been allowed to carry guns on campus.

Ironically, a bill that would have required colleges in Virginia to allow Right-to-Carry permit holders to exercise that right on campuses failed in committee not long before the Virginia Tech tragedy.

After that crime, four states proposed bills to allow concealed firearm license holders to carry on college campuses. Such bills failed in Alabama and South Carolina, but [as of December 2007] a bill is still pending in Michigan and Ohio.

Additionally, Louisiana's legislature defeated a proposed ban on firearms in college dorms and Maine rejected legislation that would have allowed colleges to prohibit firearms.

Rising School Violence

While lawmakers delay, debate and defend the status quo—in which college students basically are accorded the status of second-class citizenship—too many of those students are becoming victims of crime. In a one-week period in late September [2007] alone:

- A Delaware State University freshman was arrested for shooting two fellow students;

- An armed man on the University of Wisconsin campus "said he wished to commit suicide or be killed by police";

- A St. John's University freshman was arrested while wearing a George Bush mask and carrying a rifle at the New York college;

- An Ole Miss junior was shot to death;

- A junior at Tufts University in Massachusetts was robbed at gunpoint;

- And a University of Memphis junior was murdered.

Yet despite proclaiming their intention to stop "gun violence," the gun-ban lobby doesn't seem to have much sympathy for the victims of college campus disarmament. In response to a question regarding the empty holster protest, Peter Hamm, spokesman for the Brady Campaign, mocked, "You don't like the fact that you can't have a gun on your college campus? Drop out of school."

Students Fight Back

Not to be thwarted, however, some college students aren't giving up the fight as easily as the gun-ban lobby would hope.

When a friend proposed the idea of carrying empty holsters to show how lawful students had been disarmed, Michael Flitcraft, a 23-year-old sophomore at the University of Cincinnati, says he took the idea and ran with it. Soon dozens of students, and ultimately over 100 colleges, joined in the empty holster protest.

While drawing attention to the injustice of denying college students their constitutional rights, the protest also helped educate the public and open a constructive dialog on many campuses. "People are under the impression that this is going to suddenly put guns in the hands of college students," said Scott Lewis, a media coordinator for Students for Concealed Carry on Campus. "We have to explain that, 'No, this isn't going to change the laws on who can get a gun, and it's not going to make it legal to carry a gun while under the influence. It's just going to give people on college campuses the same rights that they already have anywhere else.'"

"I had somebody tell me, 'I'd just be terrified if I knew somebody was carrying a gun.' So I asked them, 'Why?'" said Jay Adkins, a senior at East Tennessee State University who helped organize the empty holster protest at his school. "They had this idea that guns would just randomly go off, or that people would break out into gunfights all the time," Adkins said. "But when you confront them with the facts that people do this in regular society every day, all the time, and nothing happens, they realize that college students can be just as responsible as any other adults. We're all adults. We just want people to realize that we don't suddenly become less responsible when we walk onto a campus."

Even if the media are biased in their coverage—the protest did draw some very negative press comments—many involved believe the publicity helps their cause more than the bias hurts it. "If it's big enough to get the media's attention and warrant a story," said Flitcraft, "then it's going to get the word out. And that can only help."

School Security Programs Are Not Enough

In the wake of the mass murders at Virginia Tech, colleges have adopted various official responses while basically steering away from any serious, open-minded discussion of the firearms option.

Several schools now hold exercises akin to fire drills simulating a killer on campus. Some have fitted locks to classroom doors to keep killers at bay. New Jersey state Senator Barbara Buono plans legislation requiring a lock on every college and school classroom door in the state. Virginia Tech installed sirens that, ironically, got their first use on the day of the April 16 [2007] tragedy.

Technology companies are now selling schools mass notification systems based on e-mail, text-messaging, phone calls, RSS computer feeds, PA systems and digital billboards. One such company, Omnilert LLC, reported that the number of schools using its systems jumped from 25 to over 200 after the Virginia Tech tragedy.

For its part, the International Association of Campus Law Enforcement Administrators—whose members bank on being the only armed presence on campus—has warned that allowing students who have Right-to-Carry permits to carry on college grounds "has the potential to dramatically increase violence on our college and university campuses."

Indeed, despite assurances from some university authorities that everything is on the table when it comes to campus security, the options offered almost never include the only option that can even the odds by meeting force with equal force—good people carrying firearms to protect themselves against violent criminals.

Banning Guns Leaves Students Vulnerable

Though the gun-ban lobby will never admit it, and the anti-gun media are loath to report it, even though guns are banned at schools throughout most of the United States, firearms in the hands of peaceful, ordinary citizens have proven decisive in stopping some school shootings.

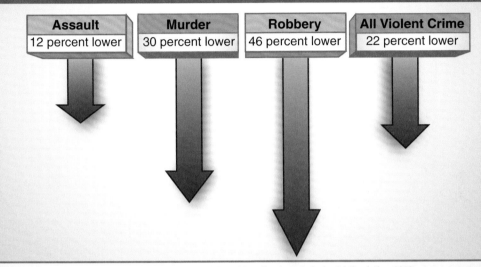

Concealed Weapons Lead to Lower Crime Rates

States that allow people to carry concealed handguns in public generally have lower rates of violent crime than the national average.

Assault	Murder	Robbery	All Violent Crime
12 percent lower	30 percent lower	46 percent lower	22 percent lower

Taken from: National Rifle Association of America, Institute for Legislative Action, 2008.

- In January 2002 at the Appalachian School of Law in Grundy, Va., a 43-year-old former student walked into the offices of two faculty members and shot them to death. Hearing the gunfire, two students immediately and independently ran to their separate cars, retrieved their firearms and returned to confront the killer and hold him at gunpoint for police, preventing any further murders.

- In Pearl, Miss., after stabbing his mother to death, a 16-year-old took a rifle to his high school, killed his former girlfriend and another girl, then began firing into the crowd. The killer was leaving to continue his rampage at a nearby school when the vice principal of his high school ran off campus to his parked vehicle, retrieved his Colt .45, stopped the rampage and held the murderer for police.

- In Edinboro, Pa., after a 14-year-old shot a science teacher to death and wounded three others at a school dance in April 1998, a restaurant owner pointed a shotgun at the shooter, forced him to surrender and held the killer for 11 minutes until police arrived.

Students Should Be Able to Protect Themselves

Of course, the gun-ban lobby loves to raise the specter of minor disagreements escalating into free-for-all shootouts among Right-to-Carry permit holders. But after crying "Wolf!" for so many years as state after state adopted Right to Carry—and seeing their dire predictions fall flat each and every time—the gun-ban lobby lost its credibility.

Consequently, gun haters shifted their story line from tragedy to comedy, ridiculing Right-to-Carry permit holders as juvenile would-be John Waynes or James Bonds, before suggesting, with infinite parental patience, that things don't work like they do in the movies, and that armed good guys would never be able to shoot as well as armed bad guys.

What's worse, though, is what such mockery and derision represent: an attempt to stifle the exchange of ideas and debate about a serious issue. In other words, hardly the kinds of things one would hope to "learn" at today's "institutes for higher learning."

As Scott Lewis pointed out in the *Washington Times*, "Whenever proponents of concealed carry point to its success throughout the nation, as well as studies showing that concealed handgun license holders are significantly less likely than non-license holders to commit violent crimes, they are answered with mockery, rather than intelligent discourse. In the world of academia and intellectual free expression, some issues are apparently not open for discussion."

In the end, the issue isn't so much whether the good guys prevail, or whether free speech is upheld. What really matters is whether the God-given right of self-defense is acknowledged and respected by the powers that be.

As Andrew Dysart, a senior at Virginia's George Mason University who organized that school's chapter of Students for

Concealed Carry on Campus, argued, "There's no guarantee to know either way whether the Right to Carry could have changed anything at Virginia Tech. But I believe those students should have been allowed at least the choice to have a chance of saving themselves. That's what's at issue here: whether or not students should have that option."

EIGHT

Larger Schools Increase the Risk of School Violence

David W. Kirkpatrick

David W. Kirkpatrick is a columnist for EdNews.org and a senior education fellow at the U.S. Freedom Foundation. In the following viewpoint Kirkpatrick argues that school size is related to increased violence at school. He states that larger schools consistently have more incidents of violence than smaller schools and that schools are not responding effectively to the potential for violence. Kirkpatrick argues that large schools are more dangerous and less able to prevent violence from occurring.

Thirty years ago, one student in four said violence was a problem at their school. At one point, nearly half of the nation's students reported they were afraid to use their school's restrooms. School violence thus has a long history and efforts to counter often show little success.

Are Schools to Blame for Violence?

Fifteen times in five years violent death and injury struck at a school. Each time everyone asked why? One standard response is that too many families are dysfunctional. Yet few if any of the families of the

David W. Kirkpatrick, "Violence in the Schools," EdNews.org, September 21, 2007. Reproduced by permission.

assailants have been judged to be guilty on this count. Frequently, they don't even fit the stereotype of low-income or urban families. Many, if not most, of the assailants have come from middle- and upper-middle-class families, some from reportedly expensive homes.

But, even if the charge of family failure should be true, there is no way "society" can enter the homes of millions of families (and which families?) to determine the upbringing of their children. Even more nebulous is the response that society has lost its bearings and no longer honors the old-fashioned values. Again, even if true, it's not a helpful guide. Even the federal government with all its resources cannot control "society."

More importantly, such broad-based explanations ignore the role of the schools. While schools cannot "correct" families or society, they can improve themselves.

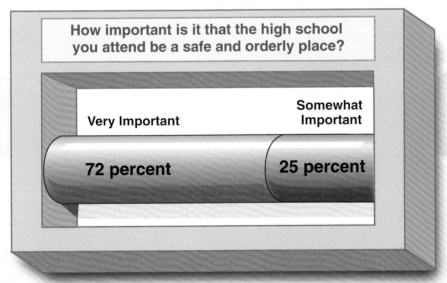

Taken from: Middle School Poll, Harris Interactive, February 14–March 5, 2007.

Even the proposed and enacted solutions within the schools tend to concentrate on security. Some "zero-tolerance" weapon policies which result in students being suspended or even expelled for such things as pointing a finger and saying "bang" seem to border on the irrational.

Other responses, while perhaps having merit, still have shortcomings. One call is for security guards. In at least one instance of school violence, one of the guards was among those shot.

Some people prescribe the use of more metal detectors. While this may have a deterrence effect, it should not lead to complacency. In one instance, two students set off a false fire alarm and, from a distance, shot at those leaving the building. Metal detectors would have been useless. In others, had the assailants faced metal detectors, the ones staffing them might have been among those shot, perhaps even the first ones to be victims.

Examining School Violence

What are some of the things many major tragedies have in common?

First, they have not occurred in inner city schools.

Second, with rare exceptions, minorities and low-income students have not been involved either as assailants nor as victims, which means race was not a factor.

In virtually every case the perpetrators indicated they were the targets of bullying, that they were loners who believed that no one cared for them or seemed to be aware they existed. These are things about which the school system can and should do something.

While it is true that these events generally occur in public schools, not in the 25,000 nonpublic schools, to frame it as a public vs. private school phenomenon is too simplistic. Violent incidents have not involved many public schools in general but mostly large ones where attendance is compulsory.

Larger Schools Are More Dangerous

Violence, at least of this magnitude, is rare in the nation's 100,000 public schools that are small. More to the point, and often over-

Some experts say that larger high schools experience more violence than smaller schools because attendance is compulsory.

looked in the school choice debate, thousands of public schools whatever their size, such as magnet schools and charter schools, are schools of choice. Everyone, staff and student alike, is there voluntarily.

One federal study of charter schools concluded that the average size of new ones is 137 students—larger ones tend to be converted public schools. The average nonpublic school is also smaller than the average public one—with about 200 pupils enrolled in each of the former to 500 in the latter. Even there, averages can be misleading. It has been reported that half of all public high schools enroll more than 1,500 students; 70% have more than 1,000.

Hundreds of studies have found that large schools are less effective and more dangerous than small ones. In addition to the research, we are repeatedly given living, or dying, proof.

Why can't we learn?

NINE

Self-Defense Training Decreases the Risk of School Violence

Dave Kopel

Dave Kopel is the research director for the Independence Institute and a regular contributor to the *National Review*. In the following viewpoint Kopel argues that schools should provide self-defense training and support for teachers and students. Basic and advanced unarmed self-defense programs can help prepare students and school staff to respond appropriately to violence. Kopel also argues that teachers should be allowed to carry guns at school. Stating that the Gun-Free Schools Act has made schools an easy target for those intent on harming others, Kopel argues that allowing qualified teachers to carry guns would deter acts of violence committed at schools. Kopel concludes that self-defense training is critical for the safety of public schools.

Since the Columbine murders in 1999, several important steps have been taken to prevent or thwart school shootings. Much more still needs to be done.

The good news is that, since Columbine, police tactics in school attacks have dramatically changed. At Columbine, the armed "school resource officer" refused to pursue the killers into the building, and kept himself safe outside while the murders were going

Dave Kopel, "The Resistance," *National Review Online*, October 10, 2006. Copyright © 2006 by National Review, Inc., 215 Lexington Avenue, New York, NY 10016. Reproduced by permission.

on inside. Even after SWAT teams arrived, and while, via an open 911 line, the authorities knew that students were being methodically executed in the library, the police stood idle just a few yards outside the library.

To this day, the authorities in Jefferson County, Colorado, have successfully covered up who made the decision that the police would stand idle.

Lessons from Columbine

Fortunately, police tactics have changed dramatically since that disgraceful day. Now, the standard police response to an "active shooter" is immediate counter-action. For example, at a March 2001 attack on Santana High School in Santee, California, the police response was immediate, and saved lives. It was the first time ever that a school shooting had been met with prompt police counter-action.

A second form of progress post-Columbine has been in greater news media responsibility. *Time* and *Newsweek* put the Columbine killers on the front cover—giving them precisely the sort of posthumous infamy which motivates many mass murderers. As Clayton Cramer has documented, massive publicity given to mass murderers plays a significant role in encouraging more mass murders.

In the 21st century, the mainstream media have been somewhat more responsible about focusing coverage on the victims, rather than the perpetrator. While stories are still written about perpetrators, they are less likely to be rewarded (in effect) with a big picture on the front of a magazine or newspaper.

Although the copycat effect may have been mitigated by giving perpetrators a little less publicity, it continues. Thus, schools and law enforcement should be especially vigilant . . . on future anniversaries of school shootings.

Self-Esteem and Bullying

After Columbine, there was a great push for anti-bullying programs and the like. Whether bullying was or is a major cause of shootings is debatable. Columbine killer Eric Harris likely suffered from a superiority complex; his problem was excessive self-esteem. Indeed, many criminals have excessively high self-esteem, and one cause of their criminality is the large gap between how most people see them (accurately, as mediocre losers) and their own self-image. Self-esteem programming in the schools, whatever its merits, might even be counterproductive to school safety.

One important value of anti-bullying programs, however, is that most of them strongly encourage students to come forward and report a problem. Much more so than in the pre-Columbine period, students and other community members who hear rumors or threats of a school attack have been willing to warn the authorities. There have been many attacks which have been prevented only because someone did so. The willingness of people to speak up has been the most significant post-Columbine step forward in safety, and has likely saved many dozens of lives.

Ineffective Anti-gun Laws

Compared to the Columbine aftermath, there is much less inclination among the political classes, and even much of the media, to use school murders as a pretext for irrelevant anti-gun laws. If it were actually possible to ban all guns, and confiscate all of the more than 200 million firearms in America, school killers would be deprived of their most effective weapon—since most killers don't have the skills to build bombs, and a criminal can't use a knife or sword to control two dozen people at a distance.

But it is pretty clear that the kinds of laws which were pushed after Columbine (one-gun-a-month in California, special restrictions on gun shows in Colorado and Oregon) are of little value in keeping guns away from people who plan their attacks a long period of time in advance.

Notably, Canada has adopted almost everything (and more) which American anti-gun lobbies have pushed in the United States. Yet this fall's [2006] spate of copycat school shootings began on September 13 in Canada, when Dawson College, in Montreal, was attacked by a 25-year-old man who killed one victim and wounded 19 more, putting two of them into a coma. (Fortunately, two policemen happened to be on campus, and they took immediate action, rather than waiting for a SWAT team to arrive. Their prompt and heroic boldness likely saved many lives.)

Schools Are Easy Targets

The attacks this fall highlight a problem that was forgotten in the post-Columbine frenzy. There are lots of attacks which are not perpetrated by disaffected students. We knew this in 1988, when 30-year-old Laurie Dann attacked a second-grade classroom in Winnetka, Illinois, and in January 1989, when an adult criminal named Patrick Purdy attacked a school playground in Stockton, California. Or when British pederast Thomas Hamilton killed 16 kindergarteners and a teacher in Dunblane, Scotland.

One reason why adult sociopaths so often choose to attack schools—schools to which they have no particular connection—is that schools are easy targets. It is not surprising that police stations, hunting-club meetings, stateside army bases, NRA [National Rifle Association] offices, and similar locations known to contain armed adults are rarely attacked.

Because of the spread of concealed-handgun licensing laws, now in 40 out of 50 states, whenever you walk into a place with a large crowd of people—a restaurant, a theater, a shopping mall—you can safely assume that several people in the crowd will have a license to carry a concealed handgun, and some of them are currently carrying.

Schools are one of the few places in the United States where the government has guaranteed that there will be no licensed, trained adults with a concealed firearm that could be used to resist a would-be mass murderer.

International Factors

Since this fact is apparently obvious to random psychopaths, it would be very dangerous to assume that the fact is not obvious to terrorists also. Beslan, Russia, shows that terrorists with al Qaeda connections consider schools to be good targets. There is also the danger of self-starting jihadis, such as the man who attacked the

Jewish community center in Seattle. Every Jewish school and community center should very seriously consider having at least one full-time security guard.

Israel has successfully used a combination of security guards, armed teachers, and armed escorts on field trips to protect schools from terrorist attack. Thailand is likewise allowing teachers to obtain handgun-carry licenses in southern regions where schools have been targeted by Islamic terrorists.

One confirmation of the strength of the case for allowing teachers the choice to be armed is the weakness of the arguments against it. Significantly, we have real-world tests of the policy—not only in Israel and Thailand, but also in the United States.

Carrying Concealed Handguns

Like many states, Utah enacted a concealed-handgun licensing law in 1995. Unlike most states, Utah did not make schools an exclusion zone for lawful carrying. Not only a teacher on duty, but also a parent coming to pick up a child from school, can lawfully carry a concealed handgun in a Utah school building—after, of course, passing a background check and safety training. (See Utah Code sect. 76-10-505.5. In 2003, the legislature expanded the law, by allowing principals to authorize firearms possession by individuals who did not have a concealed-handgun carry permit.)

After eleven years of experience in Utah, we now have exactly zero reported problems of concealed handgun licensees misusing guns at school, or students stealing guns from teachers, or teachers using their licensed firearms to shoot or threaten students. During this same period, we also have had exactly zero mass murders in Utah schools.

Allowing Teachers to Carry Guns at School

My proposal, however, is not that other states go as far as Utah. Rather, I simply suggest that teachers and other school employees be allowed to carry if they obtain a handgun carry permit. If a school wants to require special additional training for school carry, that's fine.

A University of Utah student carries a handgun on campus. In the eleven years since the law was passed, there have been no violations by Utah's concealed weapon licensees.

Some people who do not like the idea of teachers being armed to protect students simply get indignant, or declare that armed teachers are inconsistent with a learning environment. I suggest that dead students—and the traumatic aftermath of a school attack—are far more inconsistent with a learning environment than is a math teacher having a concealed handgun.

"Teachers don't want to carry guns!" some people exclaim. True enough, for most teachers. But there are about six million teachers in the United States, and it would be foolish to make claims about what every teacher thinks. The one thing that almost all teachers have in common is that they have passed a fingerprint-based background check, meaning that they are significantly less likely than the general population to have a criminal history.

There are plenty of teachers who have served in the military, or the police, or who have otherwise acquired familiarity with firearms. And there will be other teachers who would willingly undergo the training necessary to learn how to use a firearm to protect themselves and their students. After all, almost all the teachers in southern Thailand are Buddhists, and if some Buddhist teachers will choose to carry handguns, it would be ridiculous to claim that American teachers, as a universal category, would never exercise the choice to carry.

We know that school shootings have been stopped by armed citizens with guns. In 1997, a Mississippi attack was thwarted after vice principal Joel Myrick retrieved a handgun from his trunk. The killer had already shot several people at Pearl High School, and was leaving that school to attack Pearl Junior High, when Myrick pointed his .45 pistol at the killer's head and apprehended him. A few days later, an armed adult stopped a school rampage in Edinboro, Pennsylvania.

The Gun-Free Schools Act

It is commonly, but incorrectly, believed that the federal Gun-Free School Zones Act creates an insurmountable barrier to arming teachers. Not so. The GFSZA has a specific exemption for persons who have a concealed handgun carry permit from the state where the school is located, if the state requires a background check before issuance of a permit. It is state laws, not the federal GFSZ Act, which are in need of reform to allow schools to be protected.

Self-Defense Training in Schools

Pending legal reform, there are several steps that school districts can take to improve school safety. Almost all teachers spend several days a year in continuing professional education programs. Every school district should begin, at least, offering self-defense training as an option to teachers on "in-service" days.

These programs should explain the critical importance of decisive action by teachers in the very first moments when an armed intruder has entered a room. The faster that students get out, the more lives that can be saved. Allowing an intruder to take control of the room, and line students up, or tie them up, is extremely dangerous. If students flee immediately (especially if the room has at least two exits), the criminal will have a much harder time obtaining control and taking hostages.

Undoubtedly, the criminal might begin shooting immediately. But if the victim is moving and is constantly getting further from the shooter, it is much harder for the shooter to deliver a critical hit. In contrast, when the victims are stationary and under the shooter's control, the killer has an easy time delivering a fatal head shot from a foot away. At Columbine, some fleeing students were wounded, some of them very seriously. But almost all the fatalities were the result of up-close executions of stationary victims.

Defensive training for teachers can also include how quickly to disarm a person with a gun, especially when his attention is distracted. This can be a dangerous move, to be sure, and it does not always work. If it does, perhaps everyone's lives can be saved. If it does not, the killer has no greater power than if the move were never attempted.

Supporting Advanced Self-Defense for Teachers

At a more advanced level, there are programs such as Krav Maga ("contact combat")—a technique of unarmed self-defense currently used by some U.S. police departments, and the Israeli Defense Forces. It was originally created by Jews in Bratislava, during the 1930s, for self-defense against anti-Semitic thugs who might have weapons. Every school district should offer to pay half the tuition for a teacher who takes classes in Krav Maga or similar programs. Introductory versions of these programs could also be offered for free on in-service days.

Of the teachers who would never choose to carry a firearm, some would choose to carry non-lethal defensive sprays. Basic training in defensive spray-use takes an afternoon. Schools could offer more sophisticated training as well, focused on the situations most likely be encountered in a school.

Pepper sprays are not always a panacea (they don't work on some criminals, especially ones who eat a lot of spicy foods), but they can save lives. While a predator is writhing in excruciating pain, he will lose control of the situation, allowing students to flee, and giving the teacher a good chance of taking the gun.

Self-Defense Training for Students

And what about self-defense for students? Incorporating several days of self-defense into the annual physical education curriculum would be sensible anyway, even if there were no problems with school shootings. Self-defense training will make students less vulnerable at isolated bus stops, and everywhere else. The core of all self-defense training is greater awareness of one's environment, so that a person can get away from potential trouble before it becomes actual trouble.

Self-defense training also teaches that it is dangerous to let a criminal take control of your surroundings; even if a criminal is pointing a gun at you, you are probably better off to try running away, than to let him put you in a car where he can transport you to an isolated location.

Teachers and students would also learn that it is sometimes better to submit; if you can surrender your purse to a mugger, and protect yourself from injury, that is often the safe choice. We know, however, than when an armed criminal attempts to take over a school, there is no realistic hope that the criminal will be satisfied with stealing some money.

Knowing When to Act

Consider a 12th grade classroom containing 15 healthy males, several of whom are athletes. If the males rush the perpetrator en masse, some of them might be shot, but it is also likely that the perpetrator would be quickly subdued, all the more so since most school shooters are not physically powerful. The school shooting in Springfield, Oregon, ended when several brave students, including wrestler Jake Ryker, rushed the shooter; Ryker was shot, but recovered.

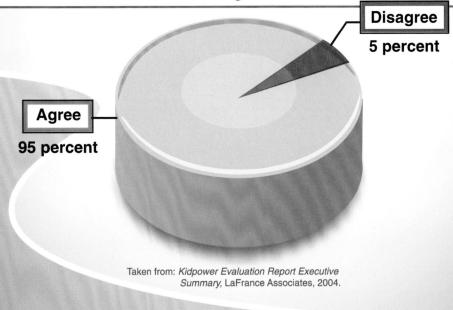

A majority of parents agree that children are safer as a result of participating in self-defense training.

Disagree
5 percent

Agree
95 percent

Taken from: *Kidpower Evaluation Report Executive Summary*, LaFrance Associates, 2004.

To some people, the notion that teachers like Joel Myrick or students like Jake Ryker should engage in active resistance is highly offensive, and the idea that teachers and students should be encouraged to learn active resistance is outrageous.

Our nation has too many people who are not only unwilling to learn how to protect themselves, but who are also determined to prevent innocent third persons from practicing active defense. A person has the right to choose to be a pacifist, but it is wrong to force everyone else to act like a pacifist. It is the policies of the pacifist-aggressives which have turned American schools into safe zones for mass murderers.

School shootings are the ultimate form of bullying, and long experience shows that the more likely and more effective the resistance, the less the bullying.

If a trained teacher carries a concealed defensive tool, such as pepper spray, there is no downside except an offense against the self-righteous sensibilities of pacifist-aggressives. Except for criminals, everyone would be a lot safer—and not just at school—if teachers and students were encouraged to learn at least basic unarmed self-defense.

TEN

Youth Leadership Programs Decrease the Risk of School Violence

Lex T. Eckenrode

Lex T. Eckenrode is the chief executive officer of the Virginia Police Chiefs Foundation. In the following viewpoint Eckenrode argues for the implementation of student leadership training as a way of preventing violence in schools. He discusses the success of Virginia's Commonwealth Youth Conference for Leadership Effectiveness (CYCLE) program. Eckenrode presents the CYCLE program as a model for schools that want to begin involving student leaders in violence prevention. Effective student leadership training focuses on self-leadership and problem solving in relation to issues such as gangs, bullying, and drugs. Eckenrode states that student leadership programs can create opportunities for understanding and communication between students and authority figures. He concludes that these programs can lead to decreased violence in schools.

According to the Center for the Study and Prevention of Violence, as reported in 2006, guns caused nearly 80 percent of all violent deaths in schools. Recalling the shooting at Columbine High School in Colorado in 1999 and the others that followed on its heels, the senseless tragedy on the campus of Virginia Tech on April 16, 2007, has renewed the United States' sense of urgency in determining how best to confront school violence. Can the law enforcement community prevent these situations or, at the least, provide school-age students with the tools to assist authorities in early detection of violence-prone students?

In a 2006 article titled "Preventing School Violence and Reducing the Frequency of Disturbing Threats," author Mark D. Lerner, Ph.D., chairman of the National Center for Crisis Management and president of the American Academy of Experts in Traumatic Stress, states that in order to prevent school violence,

> We must help our children and adolescents to develop and enhance their communication and problem-solving skills. We must teach them how to actively listen and to empathize when relating with others. We must help our children to understand the importance of articulating their feelings about themselves and for others, and to know that it is okay to err on the side of caution when expressing concerns about others. We must regularly remind them that they can turn to their parents and/or school support personnel who will take the time to listen and respond to them.

Lerner goes on to say that school violence can be stemmed by helping children to understand which of their behaviors cause others to become angry, making them aware of how negative statements about themselves promote frustration and how positive statements generate feelings of sincerity and compassion. He emphasizes that the actions, moral code, and compassion of adults will help set the standard for children. In other words, if adults give them the tools to cope, they will become more responsible, compassionate, and communicative; they will be better problem solvers and better leaders, have more self esteem, and become less frustrated and less likely to turn to violence to solve their problems.

Positive Youth Leadership Against School Violence

Following the shootings at Columbine and other schools, most police departments around the country began to review and revise their tactical response strategies to these tragically violent events. This trend included police agencies in Virginia as well. Whereas initial discussions centered on school violence, Virginia police chiefs quickly moved beyond addressing school violence as a single issue. Instead, they broadened the discussion to include educating teens to take positive leadership roles in their schools and communities. The Commonwealth Youth Conference for Leadership Effectiveness (CYCLE) was born of these discussions. Through a partnership between the Virginia Police Chiefs Foundation (VPCF) and the Pamplin College of Business at Virginia Tech, CYCLE was developed to focus not just on school violence but on many of the social issues confronting teens today.

School districts, through programs like CYCLE, are providing teens with personal leadership skills to help them make appropriate decisions throughout their lives.

Although the Columbine tragedy served as the catalyst for the CYCLE program, other, more recent incidents have proven that Columbine was not a one-time, isolated event—the threat of school violence is imminent. In January 2006, police and school officials uncovered and thwarted a plot by several teens involving two Albemarle County, Virginia, high schools, near Charlottesville, that was eerily similar to Columbine. Other states as well have had comparable incidents—both of violence and of attempts thwarted. And, of course, no one will forget the senseless Virginia Tech massacre in April of this year [2007]. Because of ongoing threats of school violence, youth leadership programs like CYCLE are perhaps more important than ever.

The CYCLE Program

The VPCF created and implemented a youth leadership education program for rising 10th-graders from around Virginia that provides teens with skills in personal leadership that will equip them to make more effective and appropriate decisions throughout their lives, as individuals and as members of a team. This program is designed to help teens focus on what they can control, developing their leadership skills and building their self-esteem. CYCLE allows students to work with other teens to learn about different cultures, gender differences, personalities, and how best to work together. It provides them with the tools to enhance their learning process, expand opportunities, increase potential, and become good leaders, giving back to the community.

This program strives to promote an environment where future leaders can learn and embrace the values of U.S. diversity. VPCF representatives were emphatic that the target audience be average teens with leadership potential but who have not been given the opportunities to which other students have had access through the school system and other public and private programs. Many teens with high grade point averages (GPAs) have opportunities to enhance their skills in a multitude of areas, and underachieving teens are provided with opportunities to make life-altering changes if they decide to do so. However, the foundation uncovered few programs focused on the group in the middle. "Average" teens often fall into the wrong crowd and can become part of the problem themselves. These are the teens who could go either way, who could easily slip through the cracks and turn to a life of crime, gang involvement, or violence.

As a result of this, CYCLE's curriculum directs leadership lessons at the "average" teen, focusing on good decision making, communication skills, diversity, good citizenship, and issues of violence and anger management. These are the skills about which Lerner speaks in his article on preventing school violence. Upon completion of the program, participants are able to gain an understanding of their leadership potential, demonstrate a better understanding of self and how to relate others, demonstrate effective communication to support positive interactions, demonstrate problem analysis skills to assist in decision making, understand the value of teamwork, and understand the individual's role in our communities and society.

Teens are taught self-leadership by a team of five Virginia Tech college juniors/seniors majoring in business, typically with a leadership minor, at Virginia Tech's Pamplin College of Business in Blacksburg. CYCLE's curriculum is supplemented with the textbook *The 7 Habits of Highly Effective Teens*, by Sean Covey. All college students directing the program—known as residential instructional counselors (RICs)—undergo a background check as well as an extensive training program conducted by Virginia Tech. RICs give teens case studies and situations to analyze and apply their new skills and put them in teams to discuss and present their solutions to such major problems as gang violence, bullies, drugs, alcohol, guns, and mean-spirited behavior. The desired outcome is a population of adolescents who, by virtue of acquired self-leadership skills, will reject violence and the use of illegal substances and encourage similar behavior among their peers. In addition, the program promotes a healthy relationship between students and law enforcement officers, increasing opportunities for understanding and communication between these two groups.

How the CYCLE Program Works

First and foremost, CYCLE is not directed at one or two areas of delinquent behavior but rather focuses on all of life's issues and making good choices. In Lerner's article, he states that "children lack interpersonal communication, coping, and problem solving skills to meet the challenges of our new world," one reason why an increasing number of them act-out feelings of anger and frustration in dangerous attention-seeking ways, "self-medicate" with alcohol and other substances, and commit suicide at a higher rate than ever before. Lerner states that "we must work toward improving communication in order to prevent violent school-based tragedies . . . through a multimodal approach." CYCLE is an effective approach that teaches, among other things, interpersonal communication, coping skills, and problem-solving strategies. In addition, the program offers the following benefits:

- CYCLE is a partnership of the local police agency, the local high school, students, and their parents or guardians.

- The program is a week-long educational course, not a summer camp or a "typical" conference, where learning is a directed activity and RICs monitor and assess individual and group outcomes.

- It is designed for "average" youths, those often overlooked by other programs targeting "at-risk" or academically "gifted" students.

- Program attendance is limited to rising 10th-grade students, both male and female, from ages 13 to 15. According to the Virginia Department of Juvenile Justice, the percentage of juveniles admitted into a Virginia detention home in 2006 more than doubled from age 14 to age 17. For this reason, CYCLE's target audience of teens age 13–15 is critical to the success of this program and to these teens' futures.

- Students are nominated for CYCLE participation by a police officer or their school resource officer.

- Students must have at least a 2.0 GPA and no major infractions on their disciplinary record.

- The local chief of police personally endorses each student application, and local police officers transport teens selected to attend CYCLE to and from the Virginia Tech campus.

Unique Interaction with Leadership Mentors

One of the other unique aspects of this program is the interrelationship among CYCLE students, RICs, and the police officers/school resource officers (SROs) who attend the sessions. Teens attend CYCLE first and foremost to learn about themselves and their potential leadership roles. But throughout the week, they also develop better communication skills with law enforcement officers and authority figures. Therefore, CYCLE fully utilizes both the RICs and the police officers/SROs to further this developing relationship.

While the students are on the campus, the RICs accompany them at all times, and three police officers attend each session with the teens. Officers and RICs stay in the dorms with the students and escort them to all events outside of the dorms, including classes, meals, and recreational activities. Other law enforcement officials from throughout Virginia visit with the teens each week of the program. In addition, the Virginia Tech Police Department patrols the campus, buildings, and dorms regularly. These measures provide these teens with the opportunity to interact positively with law enforcement officers, and the program enhances communication between these two groups long after the students graduate from CYCLE.

Benefits of Student Leadership Training

The long-term benefits of program participation reach beyond the individual teen who attends. Because the program is geared toward rising 10th-graders, CYCLE allows students to share the lessons they learned with other teens and to have a continuing influence in their schools and communities for three years after completing the program. Hopefully, these students are more likely to communicate suspicious behavior of classmates to SROs or teachers, become positive role models to other students in the school, and exhibit leadership abilities during difficult school-related situations than they were before attending the program.

The seeds CYCLE plants bear fruit not only upon completion of the program, and not just in three years' time, but maybe even more so as these teens become members of our adult community. As they assume their new roles in the coming years as working members of society and perhaps as parents, they will put to good use the life lessons they learn at programs such as CYCLE in their communities, in the workplace and even in their homes as they raise their children. Building a good foundation is the key to stability and success—the VPCF believes CYCLE is helping to do just that.

Evaluating the Results

In only six years of operation, CYCLE has exceeded the expectations of the VCPF, its board, and many others. Feedback from students, parents, counselors, SROs, and police chiefs has included many positive reports of the impact CYCLE is having not only on the youths attending but also on their peers and schools.

The evaluation plan for CYCLE's effectiveness in developing self-directed leaders includes both objective and subjective components: pretraining and posttraining written evaluation of the participants' attitudes toward personal accountability and self-leadership, follow-up interviews with CYCLE participants conducted by staff and counselors following CYCLE training, and direct feedback from students and parents.

In addition, in June 2005 staff at Virginia Tech completed a longitudinal survey of 2002–2004 CYCLE graduates. Because the 2002 CYCLE graduates were high school seniors in the 2004–2005 academic year, information was sought about the impact of their CYCLE experience and their use of skills learned during their CYCLE session. Another survey was conducted in the summer of 2007, and the results are currently being tabulated; the information gathered will be used to update the CYCLE program as needed and assist in training counselors and SROs.

Racial and ethnic diversity is also measured. Despite the fact that the CYCLE application does not request or require racial, ethnic, or gender identifiers, the program has always represented racial and ethnic diversity. In previous years, minority participation has been consistently reported at between 30 and 45 percent. In 2006, the numbers were consistent with prior years, with minorities making up 32 percent of attendees. To increase minority participation, the foundation continues to work with police officers/SROs, teachers, and guidance counselors to increase nomination and participation of minority students.

Much of CYCLE's evaluation data is anecdotal and not statistical. Part of the difficulty in compiling statistical data is that CYCLE's written evaluation forms are anonymous. Since some of the evaluation questions deal with sensitive subjects such as attitudes about sex, use of alcohol and illegal substances, as well as

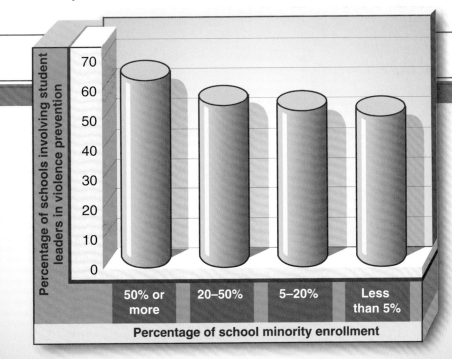

Involving Student Leaders in Violence Prevention

Schools with larger percentages of minority students are more likely to involve student leaders in violence prevention programs.

Percentage of schools involving student leaders in violence prevention

| 50% or more | 20–50% | 5–20% | Less than 5% |

Percentage of school minority enrollment

Taken from: National Center for Education Statistics, September 2007.

behavior modifications and related matters, evaluations do not require students to submit their names; this helps to ensure honest responses from student participants. This anonymity also makes it more challenging to track these individuals after they leave high school, should the foundation wish to conduct postsecondary evaluations. Acknowledging the need for additional statistical data, the foundation plans to focus future evaluation strategies to address this issue and enhance program evaluation.

Investing in Student Leaders

Each year, the foundation accepts a total of 125 students, all rising 10th graders ages 13–15, into one of five weeklong CYCLE courses—25 students per session. The cost per student is $750, which covers tuition, instructional fees, course materials, lodging, meals, and recreational activities.

For some teens, one wrong decision or one bad choice could result in law enforcement intervention, a court date, or possibly incarceration. CYCLE as a prevention program is far more cost effective than allowing these teens to become products of the juvenile justice system. The costs of juvenile homes and incarceration are ever increasing. According to the Virginia Department of Juvenile Justice, in Virginia the total cost to hold one juvenile in a detention facility or detention home is more than $100,000. Since the inception of CYCLE in 2002, 676 teens have graduated. If the program's message reaches only one or two of those students, the financial savings are still tremendous compared with the cost of sending those one or two teens to a detention facility.

The VPCF offers the program at no cost to the teens or their families. Instead, the foundation relies upon the support of police agencies, businesses, concerned citizens, and public and private grants to fund the program, as well as fund-raisers and raffles to raise awareness and financial support for CYCLE. Many CYCLE students would not have been able to attend if they had been required to pay all or even part of the expenses.

The foundation continually seeks grants and donations to help cover the costs of this program so that it may continue to offer the program to students at no charge. As the VCPF is a U.S. Internal Revenue Service–designated 501(c) (3) organization, charitable donations to it are tax deductible to the extent allowed by law.

A Model Program

As the old adage states, "If you are not part of the solution, you're part of the problem." Clearly, CYCLE and similar youth programs are not the only solution, but they can still address the problem—and provide a worthwhile opportunity for these teens. If responsible parties try nothing to stem the tide of school violence, then no progress will be made against this frightening trend. Perhaps there is no single answer to solving the dilemma of school violence, guns in school, and student driven rampages on school campuses. As Lerner points out in his article,

> It is important to understand what factors may be causing school-based tragedies. Similarly, it would be helpful to comprehend the ideation [thoughts] of people who make disturbing threats. Ultimately, research will help us to understand the causative factors and the effects of specific interventions. However, like many events in a rapidly shifting zeitgeist [cultural climate], we must take initial thoughtful, realistic, and logical steps to respond to the problems that we are facing in our schools by developing effective prevention and response strategies.

> If society can give teens better tools to manage their own self-esteem and accept responsibility for the consequences of their actions, and if it can provide opportunities for increased communication, cooperation with authority figures, and unlocking their leadership potential, it may be possible to deescalate or even prevent future incidents of school violence. Although the VCPF cannot be certain that Virginia's CYCLE program directly prevents violence in schools, it is clear that Virginia's police chiefs have the courage, wisdom, and vision to invest in teens' well-being by proactively seeking solutions to curb this disturbing trend.

ELEVEN

Parents and Schools Working Together Can Reduce School Violence

Alina Makhnovetsky

Alina Makhnovetsky is an independent journalist and contributor to *LifeStyle* magazine. In the following viewpoint Makhnovetsky argues that school violence can be prevented through the combined efforts of schools and parents working together. She discusses several cases of violence in Pennsylvania schools and outlines violence prevention programs of the state's various school districts. Makhnovetsky states that bullying is one of the primary causes of school violence and that students are sometimes influenced by information found on the Internet. She concludes that improved communication between parents and schools, parents and students, and students and teachers can effectively prevent school violence.

Every morning, Jordan Malerman takes a yellow school bus to Bala Cynwyd Middle School. But one day last month, one daily ride became a gruesome reminder of the violence and bullying that has accelerated in schools all across the nation, when a knife was discovered taped to the bus's back door. It was a shocking revelation to kids who journey together everyday: Was the knife that of a stranger or was it placed there by a fellow student?

Today, children are faced with violent situations never before imagined. There was a stabbing at Bensalem High School, a suicide at Springfield Township High School and a Columbine-like plot planned by a jolted and bullied former-student of Plymouth Whitemarsh High School. Also facing local schools are bomb threats, stolen jackets, fights and even cyber bullying. In short, Montgomery County districts have been alarmed [by] the actions of students in and out of school.

Addressing School Violence

In the wake of numerous school attacks across the nation, Bruce L. Castor, Montgomery County's District Attorney, convened a School Safety Committee of law enforcement professionals to make recommendations to retain a safe environment within schools. The School Safety Committee Report—a thirteen-page detailed document—listed specific recommendation to be implemented by each District of Montgomery County, as individual school boards, not the County, govern each.

The document listed such safety measures as added security personnel, reduced open doors accessible to the outside and ensuring those remaining open are monitored by staff, random locker searches, surveillance equipment (budget permitting), and uniforms. "After that report was drafted we invited school districts to participate in constructing the final draft. We issued that final report last summer [2007] to every school district, private school and college in the county," said District Attorney Castor. "But the County has no power to compel schools to enforce these policies."

Violence Prevention Strategies

Before the school year started, Wissahickon School District took additional security measures, requiring students to carry only clear or mesh book bags while at school. Although students are allowed to carry any type of school bag into the school, while changing classes the guidelines only allow these clear or mesh bags within the building, and a small bag for private items. The tactic was designed to prevent theft and to steer students away from bringing inappropriate or expensive items, such as iPods, to school.

Other districts also took action. After learning about the planned attack at Plymouth Whitemarsh High School, the Colonial School District has cultivated an even stronger relationship with local law enforcement, exploring such safety devices as electronic mantraps and security cameras. The district is also working on a new visitor registration system, which will scan the visitor's driver license and perform a background check.

"If the system proves to be viable and effective it will be implemented in all of the District buildings," said David M. Sherman, Colonial School District Community Relations Coordinator. "The district is also researching the viability of including a police resource officer in the high school." This was one of the recommendations of the District Attorney Committee.

Montgomery County Commissioners have also activated a wireless silent alarm system, essentially a panic button, which in the case of an emergency provides the responding officers with detailed floor plans of each school. The button will aide the school faculty in discreetly alarming the local law enforcement during an emergency. The Countywide Law Enforcement Alerting and Safety System or CLASS was recently demonstrated in Norristown. The added security was created in light of recent tragedies, most notably the shooting at West Nickel Mines School in Lancaster County, although Montgomery County has not been without incidents.

Anti-bullying Programs

Each district has also adopted extensive outreach programs and services to abolish bullying, which according to National Bureau of Justice statistics affects at least 14 percent of students, with no differences detected between public and private schools.

"There is a standard open-door policy, peer mediations, a hotline for advice or concerns and ongoing risk programs that have been in-place and evaluated. We have had for several years an ongoing process that is continually evolving as far as actions and programs that are designed to deal with how people deal with their emotions and how they deal with conflict," explained John Armato, Pottstown School District's Community Relations Director.

Lower Merion School District has been actively addressing their anti-bullying regulations. "They did tighten down on the whole bullying thing recently to try and give the kids a chance or way to protect themselves and stop if they felt bullied," said Dana Hessernan, mother of Bala Cynwyd Middle School 8th-grade student Jordan Malerman.

"I feel confident that things will change. We've had [an] auditorium meeting and our principal has came out and said that we've had bullying problems and kids were getting hurt, and it basically won't be tolerated," said Malerman. "There is still bullying, but there is a lot less then there used to be. I think if they could get more aides walking around the halls during when classes change, that would make me feel safe. A lot of people are messing around and things get stolen at that time, but it does seem the aides are doing a little more now, before they used to just ignore things, but now they are actually coming up and stopping kids from doing certain things."

Improving School Security

Added security personnel has also been one of the recommendations of the committee, and most districts reported working trained professionals into their school budgets, as well as accepting volunteers.

"I feel currently, other than putting in metal detectors, they've done what they can. You're always going to have the one or two cases of where a child is unstable or the parent is unstable or the combination of the two, that's going to bring about episodes or issues, like we've had recently," said Hessernan.

"It is not unusual for a student to share a concern with a member of a professional staff and we encourage that; if you look at a definition of what education should be, that is a part of it," said Armato.

"There has to be a good relationship between the parents and their child as well as a relationship with the faculty at school," agrees Colleen Longstreth, whose children attend schools in the Abington School District. Longstreth's children attended a similar anti-bullying auditorium meeting at their school. "At this point, I feel comfortable, but I guess I haven't had to think about that, because they have not had any trouble thus far," confessed Longstreth.

Both mothers moved to their respective neighborhoods for the school district. "I know they are doing everything in their power, I feel we are in a safe area, but I could be wrong," said Hessernan.

School Violence Is Difficult to Prevent

Overall, short of having county schools resemble airport security, the school districts seem to be doing everything possible to ensure safety for children, yet school violence seems to still plague the news.

"Would have a metal detector prevented what happened in Bensalem High School?" asked Armato, referring to the late November [2007] stabbing of a 15-year-old inside a boy's bathroom on the first floor of Bensalem High School. The teen was stabbed in the abdomen with scissors.

In such cases, the school districts seem powerless. The districts are also powerless to controlling cyber bullying, another side effect of growing up in the technologically advanced generation. In recent news, a teen committed suicide after classmates teased her insatiably on the net. Also in 2007, Montgomery County was in the national news spotlight with a case that fully encompassed the national epidemic of school violence, bullying, parental supervision and Internet.

Fourteen-year-old Dillon Cossey was accused of planning a massacre attack on his former schoolmates and bullies at Plymouth Whitemarsh High School. Cossey was taken into custody to await trial, and at press time, District Attorney Castor was still deliberating whether to try him as an adult. Cossey's mother was also taken into custody, for purchasing a .22 caliber gun for her son, unaware he planned to retaliate against his abusers.

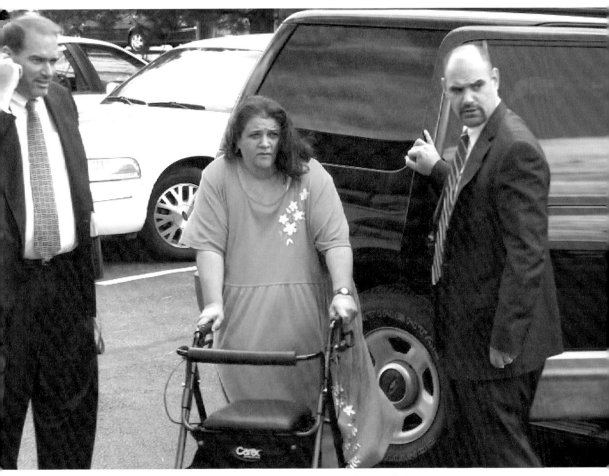

Michelle Cossey, mother of Dillon Cossey, was arrested for buying her son a .22 caliber handgun with which he planned to retaliate against his schoolmates.

Speaking Up to Prevent Violence

The case garnered national exposure once Lewis Bennett III, a student Cossey had confided in, revealed the boy's plans. Bennett notified his parents and the family called the authorities before Cossey could execute his attack, which would have likely included three homemade grenades packed with black powder.

Bennett was personally thanked by President George W. Bush for speaking out. "The danger of remaining silent outweighs the mindset of 'not wanting to be a snitch or get involved,'" said

District Attorney Castor. "We must encourage students to tell [their parents] whenever they hear of possible threats to school security. He did the right thing."

School Violence and the Internet

Cossey, a reserved boy, has been home schooled, and seem[ed] to find solace on the Internet, specifically among other alienated teens support groups, such as one dedicated to "heroes of Columbine," the shooters Eric Harris and Dylan Klebold. His

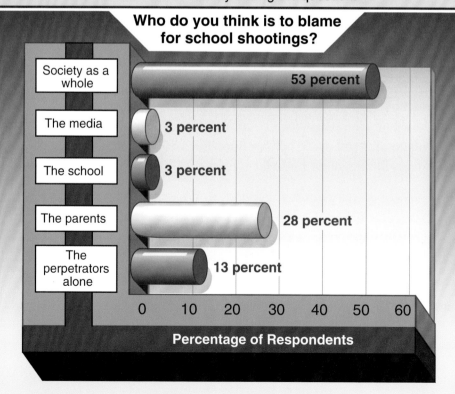

Determining Responsibility for School Violence

An online public survey examines responsibility for school violence by asking the question:

Who do you think is to blame for school shootings?

Society as a whole	53 percent
The media	3 percent
The school	3 percent
The parents	28 percent
The perpetrators alone	13 percent

Percentage of Respondents

Taken from: School Violence Poll, ParentCenter.com.

MySpace page revealed an even darker persona, a boy fascinated with violence, guns, war and school attacks, his page packed with YouTube images of violence and blood.

But the fact remains, Cossey is just one of more than 10 million members listed on a MySpace group site dedicated to preserving the memories [of] the shooters, one of which is led by 17-year-old Casandra. "It's an obsession, I think. I don't know how to explain it, I feel weird when I think about it, but I want to know what other people think of it, and why they think they did it," said Casandra of her interest in school shootings. Most of the high school senior's classmates do not know about her MySpace page or groups she belongs to. Unfortunately, Casandra's parents also have no idea that her page lists her general interests in guns, violence, school shootings and torture, featuring portraits of the Columbine shooters as her heroes and crushes. "My mom would freak and my dad wouldn't care," explains Casandra.

On the Internet, a flood of free information is immediate, vast and perhaps in the wrong hand[s] deadly. And while most parents remain in the dark, clueless about Facebook or MySpace pages, chat rooms their children visit and video games their children play, it seems not even metal detectors could protect or ensure safety in schools from [the] Internet. Although it is not fair to say that teens such as Casandra plan to harm themselves or others, at this point it seems better not [to] leave any rock unturned, and the Internet, like any powerful tool, should be handled with great responsibility and care, not only in schools, but at home.

"Jordan is not on MySpace," said Hessernan. "Jordan's Internet use is limited by me, he only goes to Web sites that I allow," confirms Hessernan. "In Lower Merion School District, they have actually banned computer games that have violence or weapons. Although I am not exactly sure how they can limit the kids, there are no weapons allowed in school, even if they are plastic, even if they are for Halloween."

District Attorney Castor feels that this is a step in the right direction, even if it is virtually impossible to control all student Internet access all of the time. "Congress must step in to regulate the Internet as the issue is of national and international scope.

The Federal Courts will have to balance free speech consideration with public safety," he said.

Parents' Involvement Can Prevent School Violence

"The more attuned everyone becomes to the environment they are in, the more [that] can be prevented," urged Armato. "Talk to your children all the time, get a sense for knowing what is going on in their lives. Parents who take time to be involved in their child's lives foster relationships that encourage open dialog, and model appropriate behavior can and do make a difference."

"Good behavior and solid moral values begin at home," agreed Sherman. "You have to be involved in your child's life, socially as well as when your child is in school," said Longstreth. "In first grade you can come in and be a mystery reader, and in that time that I spend with the kids, I talk to them a little before and after, get to know their classmates, there are also family nights and sometimes I volunteer as a lunch aide."

To better foster a safe environment, each school can forward a list of requirements to students and parents, to inspire better values, morals and conduct. Still neither the committee nor the district has the power to force their opinions. Yet it is only with combined effort that possible safety can be ensured and, as the saying goes, it takes a village. Although, our village might be filled with malls, highways, Internet and immediate gratification, it is still our village, our community, where everyone must strive to make things better.

TWELVE

Threat Assessment Decreases the Risk of School Violence

Dewey G. Cornell

> Dewey G. Cornell is a clinical psychologist, professor of education, and the director of the Virginia Youth Violence Project at the University of Virginia. In the following viewpoint Cornell argues that while schools are essentially safe, incidents of violence can be prevented through threat assessment. Cornell discusses the practice of evaluating threats of violence made at schools and gives examples of successful school threat assessment programs. He states that society's perception of school violence has been distorted by media reports of the worst school shootings. Cornell stresses that threat assessment programs can prevent these tragedies as well as less serious forms of violence, such as bullying and fighting.

Threat assessment is a procedure developed by the Secret Service that has become a standard law enforcement approach used in many different settings. Threat assessment involves identifying a threat, evaluating how serious it is, and taking action to prevent it from being carried out. Most educators were completely unfamiliar with "threat assessment" and were unprepared to implement this approach. In response, my

Dewey G. Cornell, "Student Threat Assessment," Statement to the U.S. House Committee on Education and Labor Hearing on Best Practices for Making College Campuses Safe, May 15, 2007. Reproduced by permission.

colleagues and I at the University of Virginia have developed and field-tested a threat assessment model for primary and secondary schools. I am going to talk first about the safety of our schools and then about our research on threat assessment and how it can be used to improve the safety conditions in our nation's colleges as well as our K–12 schools.

This year [2007] we have experienced tragic shootings at the Amish school in Pennsylvania and at Virginia Tech, among others. In response to such horrific events, there have been calls to increase security at our schools, and even suggestions to arm our teachers. There are recommendations to install sirens and cameras and to create high-tech warning systems to alert students to an attack. While these interventions focus on crisis response, it is critically important that our efforts concentrate on prevention strategies. Prevention cannot wait until the gunman is in your parking lot. School shootings can be prevented and I am here today to emphasize prevention.

In order to prevent violence, we have to study the problem objectively and make sure that our responses are not skewed by extreme cases. After Columbine, many schools overreacted by expanding zero tolerance programs so that students were expelled for behaviors as trivial as bringing a plastic knife to school in their lunch box. We continue to see students as young as five years old being arrested for misbehavior that would have been handled much differently ten years ago. We have to be careful that our responses are measured and reasonable.

Recognizing School Safety

First, I want to address school safety from a broader and more positive perspective. Despite recent events, the level of violent crime in our schools and colleges is low. National crime statistics demonstrate that it is safer for a student to be at school than to be at home or on the street. Crime victim research also finds that students are less likely to be harmed at school than in the community. These findings hold up for both K–12 schools and colleges. For example, the violent crime rate is lower on college campuses than off campuses and the victimization rate for college students is lower than for persons the same age who are not in college.

Furthermore, there is no upward trend of increasing violence in our schools. Over the past ten years, the rate of violence in schools and colleges has actually declined substantially.

According to the latest available data from the U.S. Department of Education (2001–2004), there were 95 murders on college campuses in the six years from 1999 to 2004, an average of 16 per year. Since there are approximately 4,200 colleges in the United States, this means the average college can expect to experience a murder on campus about once every 265 years. If you include all 2,808 murders that occurred in the surrounding community—off campus as well as on campus—the rate is much higher: about once every 9 years. This is a reflection of the much higher rate of violence in the general community.

It was tragic to have 33 deaths in one day at Virginia Tech, but according to the CDC [Centers for Disease Control and Prevention], every year more than 30,000 persons die by firearms through suicide or homicide. This is the equivalent of the Virginia Tech death toll occurring 2 to 3 times every day. This is not to minimize the tragedy of school shootings; we want the number to be zero. But if we are going to prevent these events, we have to start with placing them in a broader context.

Effective Violence Prevention for Schools

Although research demonstrates that schools are safe and that extreme acts of violence are unlikely, we do have less severe forms of violence such as bullying, fighting, and threatening behavior. These are important problems in their own right, and they are also important because they can escalate into shootings.

Fortunately, we have effective violence prevention programs for schools. There have been more than 200 controlled studies of school violence prevention programs, and we know that school-based mental health programs and counseling focused on helping students learn how to solve problems and resolve conflicts are effective. A scientific review of these studies by researchers at Vanderbilt University found that they can reduce violent and disruptive behavior by about 50 percent. If these programs were more widely used, we could identify and help troubled students before they reach the point of homicide. The main source of funding for school violence prevention is through the Office of Safe and Drug-Free Schools. Funding for this program should be protected and expanded.

Terms like "school violence" and "campus violence" are misleading because they imply that the location is the defining feature of the problem. We have had mass shootings in restaurants and shopping malls, but no one speaks about "restaurant violence" or "mall violence." The focus on location leads to unrealistic efforts to make open, public places so secure that they are no longer open or public. We cannot turn our schools into fortresses. We cannot search every backpack on college campuses.

The Virginia Tech shooting appears to be the act of an individual with severe mental illness who was paranoid, delusional, and suicidal. This shooting represents a mental health problem more than a school problem. Our nation suffers from poor insurance coverage for mental health services, and from poor communication and coordination among these services. Even when we know someone needs treatment, there is no effective mechanism to make sure the treatment is delivered and no follow-up to make sure it was effective. College campuses see a substantial number of students with serious mental health problems, yet their staffing levels and resources are focused on short term counseling.

Effective Threat Assessment for Schools

After Columbine, there was widespread demand for a checklist of characteristics that we could use to identify the next shooter. This is called profiling, and both the FBI and Secret Service have concluded that profiling is not possible for this kind of crime. The backgrounds of school shooters are too varied, and the characteristics they have in common are too general.

However, both the FBI and Secret Service observed that in almost every case the violent student communicated his or her intentions well in advance of an attack. These individuals usual-

In the wake of the Columbine High School shootings there was widespread demand for a checklist of personal characteristics that could help identify potential shooters.

ly made threats or engaged in threatening behavior that frightened others. The problem was that there was not an effective, systematic response to these threats. The FBI also observed that many potential school shootings were prevented because threats were investigated and found to be credible. In light of these findings, both the FBI and the Secret Service, in conjunction with the U.S. Department of Education, recommended that schools adopt a threat assessment approach.

Threat assessment is a standardized procedure for investigating a threat, and if the threat is a serious substantive threat, taking preventive action. At the University of Virginia we developed a set of threat assessment guidelines and we trained teams in 35 schools. Each team included a school administrator, a psychologist or counselor, and a law enforcement officer. The teams field-tested the guidelines for a year. Although serious acts of violence are rare in schools, threats are common. The school teams investigated 188 student threats of violence.

Understanding and Evaluating Threats

All threats are not the same. Some threats are just statements made in anger or in jest, or attempts to gain attention or be provocative. The first step in threat assessment is to determine whether the threat is serious, which we term substantive, or not serious or transient. Fortunately, most threats are transient and can be readily resolved with an explanation, an apology, and some counseling. About 70 percent of the threats were resolved in this manner.

The remaining 30 percent of threats were more serious, usually one student threatening to fight another student, but we had threats to shoot and stab and kill that could not be easily resolved. In these cases, our threat assessment team conducted a safety evaluation that included two components: a psychological assessment of the student and a law enforcement investigation of whether there was evidence that the person was preparing to carry out the threat. The combination of mental health and law enforcement is essential to a threat assessment.

The team takes a problem solving approach—why did this student make a threat and what can we do to reduce the risk of violence? We found students who had serious mental health problems that needed treatment. We found students who were victims of bullying and looking for a way to strike back. We found conflicts over girlfriends and boyfriends. All kinds of threats.

Every threat signals an underlying problem that should be addressed before it escalates into violence. In our follow-up study, we could not find that any of the threats were carried out. Out of 188 cases, we had just six students who were arrested and three who were expelled. This is a much better result than if the schools had used a zero tolerance approach that would have resulted in numerous expulsions. The American Psychological Association's report on zero tolerance found that school expulsions have a damaging effect on student achievement and increase the dropout rate. There is no evidence that zero tolerance makes schools safer.

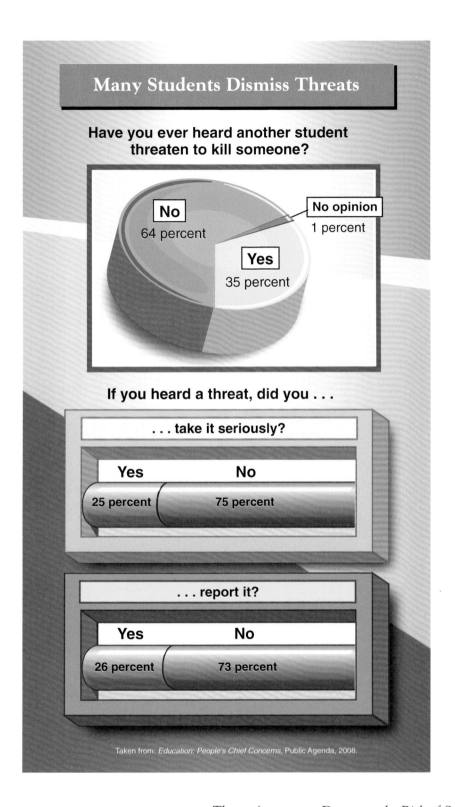

Many Students Dismiss Threats

Have you ever heard another student threaten to kill someone?

No
64 percent

No opinion
1 percent

Yes
35 percent

If you heard a threat, did you . . .

. . . take it seriously?

Yes	No
25 percent	75 percent

. . . report it?

Yes	No
26 percent	73 percent

Taken from: *Education: People's Chief Concerns*, Public Agenda, 2008.

Successful Threat Assessment

Memphis City Public Schools has adapted our model and found that they were able to resolve more than 200 threats without any known violent outcomes and again keeping almost all of the students in school. Over the past 5 years we have trained thousands of threat assessment teams in a dozen states. But we need more research on threat assessment. There has been no federal program designated to fund threat assessment research. The Secret Service has conducted threat assessment training in conjunction with the Office of Safe and Drug-Free Schools, but this has been a limited effort. We need a strong initiative to make threat assessment part of every school's comprehensive school safety plan. . . .

Threat assessment can be adapted for colleges, too, even though there are some important differences between K–12 schools and colleges. College students are adults and not under parental control. It is much easier to monitor and supervise a high school student than a college student. On the other hand, threat assessment is used in business and industry to prevent workplace violence, so these challenges can be overcome.

In closing, our educational institutions have an obligation to maintain a safe and supportive environment that is conducive to learning. Overall, our schools and colleges are safe, but in a large nation with thousands of schools, even rare events will occur with troubling frequency and skew our perceptions of safety and risk. We must avoid overreacting to rare events and make better use of prevention methods that address the ordinary forms of violence as well as the more extreme ones.

Threat assessment is a standard violence prevention approach used by law enforcement in many different settings. Our research supports the use of threat assessment in schools, but we need more research and training to make it a standard practice and to extend it to colleges.

What You Should Know About School Violence

What Is School Violence?

School violence takes many forms, making it difficult to describe in a way that includes all possible examples of violence in schools. As a result, a broad definition is normally used to discuss school violence. In general, it is identified as any action, behavior, or threat that disrupts a school's educational mission, endangers or harms students and/or school employees, or creates disorder and terror. Using this definition, school violence can involve just one or two students, in the form of bullying or fighting. Or school violence can involve an entire community, such as in the case of a school shooting or bomb threat.

Facts About School Violence

The U.S. Centers for Disease Control and Prevention (CDC) reports that:

- Youth violence is the second leading cause of death for young people between the ages of ten and twenty-four.

- The number of school-associated student deaths in the United States decreased between 1992 and 2006.

- Less than 1 percent of all murders and suicides among school-age youth occur on school grounds, on the way to or from school, or on the way to or from school-sponsored events.

According to the National School Safety Center:

- Approximately 75 percent of school-associated deaths between 1997 and 2007 involved guns.

- During that time, as many as twelve bully-related and sixteen hate-crime deaths occurred in schools.

The CDC conducted a national survey of students in grades nine through twelve in 2007, revealing that the number of students who were involved in episodes of school-associated violence was low overall:

- More than 16 percent of male students and more than 8 percent of female students were in a physical fight on school property in the twelve months before the survey.

- Nearly 6 percent of students brought a weapon (gun, knife, or club) to school on one or more days in the thirty days before the survey.

- Nearly 8 percent of students were threatened or injured with a weapon on school property one or more times in the twelve months before the surveys.

- More than 5 percent of students missed school on one or more days in the thirty days before the survey because they felt unsafe at school or on their way to or from school.

Who Is Affected by School Violence?

The effects of school violence are often different for each person, depending on his or her connection to a traumatic event. School violence affects students, teachers, and school employees, as well as their families, friends, and loved ones. Members of the general public may also experience the effects of school violence if incidents occur frequently in a particular area or if an incident is large in scale.

What Are the Effects of School Violence?

The CDC observes that some incidents of school violence cause more emotional harm than physical harm, while others can lead to serious injury or even death. According to the National Child Traumatic Stress Network, the intense fear caused by school violence can result in serious, potentially long-lasting effects on a person's physical health, mental health, and future development. Students may worry constantly about their own safety or the safety of others. Sometimes students become preoccupied with memories of a violent event or have feelings of extreme guilt or shame about what they did or did not do when the event was happening. Some students become overwhelmed by their feelings after experiencing school violence and may begin acting in self-destructive or reckless ways. Some students may talk endlessly about the traumatic event, while other students may become extremely depressed and withdrawn, refusing to talk about the event at all.

The American Academy of Pediatrics observes that students who are victims or witnesses of violence often have similar feelings or behaviors afterward, including:

- Fear or worry about being safe.
- Aggression toward others.
- Depression.
- Trouble sleeping; nightmares.
- Less independence; fear of going out alone.
- Frequent headaches or stomachaches.
- Increased anxiety.
- Eating disorders.
- Low self-esteem.
- Withdrawal from normal activities.
- Poor school performance.
- Difficulty paying attention.
- Obsessive thoughts of the event, reliving the event.
- Avoiding talking about or acknowledging the event.
- Feeling numb; having no feelings.
- Suicidal thoughts.

What You Should Do About School Violence

Prevent Violence from Occurring

The Center for the Study and Prevention of Violence provides tips and suggestions for avoiding potentially dangerous situations at school:

- Use the buddy system. Walk with other students while passing through high-risk areas on the school campus.

- Be aware. Pay attention to your surroundings while walking to and from school, and travel to and from school with other students if possible.

- Use safe spaces. If you are being threatened, bullied, or intimidated, stay close to the teachers or monitors who are on duty at lunch time, recess, and/or free periods.

- Walk away. Leave the area if other students are being verbally or physically aggressive. Get help from a teacher or other adult.

- Speak up. Tell your parents, teachers, school counselors, or other staff if you know about any potential threats or dangers at school.

- Stand up. Be confident—but not aggressive—with potential bullies.

- Telling is not tattling. Immediately inform school officials of any bullying, victimizations, and/or threats.

- Educate yourself. Take a violence prevention class, or find out how to start a violence prevention program at your school.

- Defend yourself. Learning a weaponless self-defense sport such as martial arts can help build self-confidence.

- Avoid gangs. Gang membership increases your risk of becoming involved with violence. Even if you are not in a gang, hanging out with gang members or dressing, talking, and acting like a gang member increases your risk of becoming a victim of violence.

- Avoid drugs and alcohol. Using drugs or drinking—or hanging around with those who do—increases your risk of becoming a victim of violence.

Stop Bullying

Research has shown that many incidents of school violence start with bullying. The Stop Bullying Now Campaign provides suggestions for reducing bullying at your school:

- Know your school's policy on bullying. What is your school doing to prevent bullying?

- Decide whom you will talk to if you or someone you know is bullied. Are you most comfortable asking for help from a parent, a teacher, or another adult?

- Get involved. Take part in your school's antibullying programs, or find out how to start a program if your school does not have one. Ask a teacher or other adult for help getting started.

- Be a leader. Talk with other students about bullying, and also talk with adults. Bullying can happen anywhere, and many adults understand the effects of bullying and can help with ways to keep students safe in and out of school.

If Violence Occurs

The Web site www.KidsHealth.org offers tips for staying safe in a dangerous or potentially dangerous situation, in or out of school:

- Get to somewhere safe. If you see someone with a weapon, get away as quickly and quietly as possible.

- Get help. Immediately tell an adult you trust and who

will keep your name confidential, such as a school counselor, principal, teacher, coach, or parent.

- If you cannot find an adult you trust or one who will keep your name confidential, make an anonymous phone call to your school office and report the incident. Or you can call 911 and ask to keep your identity confidential.

- Write it down. As soon as you can, write down everything you can remember about the incident, including the people involved, the type of weapon, the date and time it happened, what happened, where it happened, whether it was reported, and if so, to whom. This will help you remember in case you are asked about it later.

Recovering from Violence

Coping with the aftermath of a traumatic event can be difficult. The CDC provides these suggestions for dealing with the feelings and fears that may come up:

- Talk to an adult you trust, such as a teacher, parent or other relative, coach, or clergy member. If you are not sure whom to talk to, call a crisis intervention center or a national hotline such as 1-866-SAFEYOUTH.

- Stay active and connected to your community. Volunteering, joining a club or after-school program, or taking up a new hobby can help you handle your emotions.

- Work to make your school or community safer. Get involved with a group in your school or community, or start your own group to promote nonviolence and conflict resolution. Ask an adult for help in getting started.

- Take action. Learn how to report crimes or suspicious activities and be willing to do so.

The editors have compiled the following list of organizations concerned with the issues debated in this book. The descriptions are derived from materials provided by the organizations. All have publications or information available for interested readers. The list was compiled on the date of publication of the present volume; the information provided here may change. Be aware that many organizations take several weeks or longer to respond to inquiries, so allow as much time as possible.

Brady Campaign to Prevent Gun Violence
c/o The Brady Center to Prevent Gun Violence
1225 Eye St. NW, Ste. 1100, Washington, DC 20005
(202) 898-0792
Web site: www.bradycampaign.org

The Brady Campaign to Prevent Gun Violence is the grassroots activist affiliate network of the Brady Center to Prevent Gun Violence. It identifies itself as the largest nonpartisan grassroots organization leading the fight to prevent gun violence in the United States. Its Web site provides information and resources about issues related to gun violence, including a special section on school safety issues.

Center for the Prevention of School Violence
c/o North Carolina Department of Juvenile Justice and Delinquency Prevention
4112 Pleasant Valley Rd., Ste. 214, Raleigh, NC 27612
(919) 789-5580 or (800) 299-6054
Web site: www.ncdjjdp.org/cpsv

The Center for the Prevention of School Violence was one of the first state school safety centers in the United States, originally formed to serve schools in North Carolina. Through its Web site, the center provides information and resources nationwide, focusing on efforts that promote safer schools that are "free of fear and conducive to learning."

Children's Defense Fund
25 E St. NW, Washington, DC 20001
(202) 628-8787 or (800) 233-1200
e-mail: cdfinfo@childrensdefense.org
Web site: www.childrensdefense.org

Children's Defense Fund is a nonprofit advocacy group that identifies itself as "the voice for all the children of America" working to "ensure every child a healthy start, a head start, a fair start, a safe start, and a moral start in life and successful passage to adulthood." Its Web site includes an online library of publications on the issues and challenges facing American children today, including school safety.

Educators for Social Responsibility
23 Garden St., Cambridge, MA 02138
(617) 492-1764 or (800) 370-2515
e-mail: educators@esrnational.org
Web site: www.esrnational.org

Educators for Social Responsibility is a nonprofit organization that works with teachers and school administrators to design and implement policies for the creation of safe schools. Its Web site includes resources and information about school safety programs such as peer mediation and conflict resolution.

Justice Learning
c/o Justice Talking
Annenberg Public Policy Center
3535 Market St., Ste. 200, Philadelphia, PA 19104
(215) 898-5081
e-mail: jl_info@justicelearning.org
Web site: www.justicelearning.org

Justice Learning is a collaborative educational project of National Public Radio's *Justice Talking* program and the *New York Times*

Learning Network. Its Web site provides materials for students interested in the issues and conflicting opinions currently being debated in American society. The Web site includes articles, editorials, and debates on a range of issues related to school violence and safety policies.

National Center for Juvenile Justice
3700 S. Water St., Ste. 200, Pittsburgh, PA 15203
(412) 227-6950
Web site: ncjj.servehttp.com/NCJJWebsite/main.htm

The National Center for Juvenile Justice is a nonprofit resource center for information on topics related to all aspects of the U.S. juvenile justice system. Its Web site includes a library of research publications and statistical reports, including information on the results of school discipline policies that often channel students into the juvenile justice system.

National Child Traumatic Stress Network (NCTSN)
c/o National Center for Child Traumatic Stress
University of California at Los Angeles
11150 W. Olympic Blvd., Ste. 650, Los Angeles, CA 90064
(310) 235-2633
Web site: www.nctsnet.org

The NCTSN is a coalition of academic and community-based service centers working to improve services for children who have experienced violence or other traumatic events. Its Web site includes a library of downloadable resources on topics related to traumatic stress in children and teens; many resources are available in Spanish as well as English.

National Crime Prevention Council
2345 Crystal Dr., Ste. 500, Arlington, VA 22202-4801
(202) 466-6272
Web site: www.ncpc.org

The National Crime Prevention Council creates educational programs, publications, and educational materials to help individuals reduce and prevent crime in their communities. Its Web site includes a school safety section with tips and resources for students interested in making their school safer.

National Education Association (NEA)
1201 Sixteenth St. NW, Washington, DC 20036
(202) 833-4000
Web site: www.nea.org

The NEA is a volunteer-based organization of educators and academic professionals. The NEA works to advance the cause of public education in the United States so that every child can receive the highest quality education. Its Web site includes information about current issues in school policy development and implementation, including a section devoted to school safety.

National School Safety Center
141 Duesenberg Dr., Ste. 11, Westlake Village, CA 91362
(805) 373-9977
Web site: www.schoolsafety.us

The National School Safety Center was established by a directive from then U.S. president Ronald Reagan. The center identifies itself as "an advocate for safe, secure, and peaceful schools worldwide and as a catalyst for the prevention of school crime and violence." Its Web site covers issues related to school safety, emergency readiness, and crisis prevention. An online resource center includes downloadable fact sheets and handouts on specific school safety issues.

National Youth Violence Prevention Resource Center
PO Box 10809, Rockville, MD 20849-0809
(866) 723-3968
e-mail: NYVPRC@safeyouth.org
Web site: www.safeyouth.org

The National Youth Violence Prevention Resource Center identifies itself as a user-friendly, single point of access to U.S. federal government information on youth violence. It operates a crisis intervention hotline for youth and other victims of violence,

(866) SAFEYOUTH. Its Web site offers current information from various federal agencies for parents, youth, and other interested individuals, and links to further resources.

PAX/Real Solutions to Gun Violence
100 Wall St., 2nd Fl., New York, NY 10005
(212) 269-5100 or (800) 983-4275
e-mail: info@paxusa.org
Web sites: www.paxusa.org and www.safeschoolsweek.org

PAX is a national nonprofit organization that works to end gun violence against children. Its Web site provides information about community programs that encourage individuals to be aware of the potential for gun violence and to respond appropriately to threats of violence. PAX also sponsors a national Safe Schools Week violence prevention program and provides downloadable events and activities information for students interested in bringing the program to their schools.

SaferSanerSchools
PO Box 229, Bethlehem, PA 18016
(610) 807-9221
e-mail: usa@safersanerschools.org
Web site: www.safersanerschools.org

SaferSanerSchools is a project of the International Institute for Restorative Practices that promotes school safety through student programs such as peer mediation. Its Web site provides links to an extensive collection of online resources for alternative approaches to student discipline and school safety.

Stop Bullying Now Campaign
c/o Health Resources and Services Administration
5600 Fishers Ln., Rockville, MD 20857
e-mail: comments@hrsa.gov
Web site: www.stopbullyingnow.hrsa.gov

The Stop Bullying Now Campaign is a program of the U.S. Department of Health and Human Services, Health Resources and Services Administration. Stop Bullying Now encourages youth to be aware of bullying and its effects. Its Web site includes a series of animated videos about bullying, with tips on responding to bullies in various situations.

Students Against Violence Everywhere (SAVE)
322 Chapanoke Rd., Ste. 110, Raleigh, NC 27603
(919) 661-7800 or (866) 343-SAVE
e-mail: info@nationalsave.org
Web site: www.nationalsave.org

SAVE is a national student-based organization that teaches young people about alternatives to violence as well as conflict resolution and prevention of crime and violence. SAVE's Web site includes an extensive collection of fact sheets, statistics, information sheets, issue toolkits, and links to other online resources. Information is provided for those interested in forming a chapter at their school.

Students for Concealed Carry on Campus
e-mail: MediaTeam@ConcealedCampus.org
Web site: www.concealedcampus.org

Students for Concealed Carry on Campus is a national organization that supports the legalization of carrying properly licensed handguns in university and college campus environments. Its Web site provides facts, statistics, and information on topics such as school safety, school violence, self-defense, concealed handgun licenses, and concealed weapons permits.

Teach Safe Schools
Web site: www.teachsafeschools.org

Teach Safe Schools is a research project of the Melissa Institute for Violence Prevention and Treatment. Its mission is to "bring the results of research in violence prevention and treatment to the educators who are working diligently in our schools to ensure the safety and success of all students and faculty." Its Web site provides information on developing supportive, safe schools. A special section helps individuals evaluate current conditions at their own school and determine the appropriate steps to take to improve school safety.

What Kids Can Do
PO Box 603252, Providence, RI 02906
(401) 247-7665
e-mail: info@whatkidscando.org
Web site: www.whatkidscando.org

What Kids Can Do is a national organization that promotes positive images of youth. Its Web site includes an online library of publications and viewpoints written by young people on a range of issues related to school safety, student discipline, and school policy reform.

BIBLIOGRAPHY

Books

Kern Alexander and M. David Alexander, *The Law of Schools, Students and Teachers in a Nutshell.* St. Paul: West, 2003.

Lorraine Stutzman Amstutz and Judy H. Mullet, *The Little Book of Restorative Discipline for Schools: Teaching Responsibility, Creating Caring Climates.* Intercourse, PA: Good Books, 2005.

Louise Benson, *Scapegoating for Columbine: Collateral Damage in the War on School Violence.* Lincoln, NE: iUniverse, 2007.

Barbara Coloroso, *The Bully, the Bullied, and the Bystander: From Pre-School to High School.* New York: HarperResource, 2003.

Dewey G. Cornell, *School Violence: Fears Versus Facts.* Mahwah, NJ: Lawrence Erlbaum, 2006.

Tish Davidson, *School Conflict.* New York: Franklin Watts, 2004.

John Devine and Jonathan Cohen, *Making Your School Safe: Strategies to Protect Children and Promote Learning.* New York: Teachers College Press, 2007.

Cybelle Fox, David J. Harding, Jal Mehta, and Wendy Roth, *Rampage: The Social Roots of School Shootings.* New York: Basic, 2005.

James Garbarino, *See Jane Hit: Why Girls Are Growing More Violent and What We Can Do About It.* New York: Penguin, 2006.

Joseph Liberman, *The Shooting Game: The Making of School Shooters.* Santa Ana, CA: Seven Locks, 2006.

Erica R. Meiners, *Right to Be Hostile: Schools, Prisons, and the Making of Public Enemies.* New York: Routledge, 2007.

Tamara Orr, *Violence in Our Schools: Halls of Hope, Halls of Fear.* New York: Franklin Watts, 2003.

Rick Phillips, John Linney, and Chris Packs, *Safe School Ambassadors: Harnessing Student Power to Stop Bullying and Violence.* San Francisco: Jossey-Bass, 2008.

Kathy Sexton-Radek, *Violence in Schools: Issues, Consequences, and Expressions.* Westport, CT: Praeger, 2004.

Karen M. Sowers, *Kids and Violence: The Invisible School Experience.* Binghamton, NY: Haworth SocialWork Practice, 2004.

R. Murray Thomas, *Violence in America's Schools: Understanding, Prevention, and Responses.* Westport, CT: Praeger, 2006.

Periodicals and Internet Sources

ABC News, "Should Students Carry Concealed Guns on Campus?" February 6, 2008. http://abcnews.go.com/GMA/Storyid=430 1073.

———, "Why Girls Are Getting More Violent," March 11, 2006. http://abcnews.go.com/GMA/Health/story?id=1713709.

AlterNet, "Why Was the Illinois Shooter Allowed to Buy a Gun?" February 18, 2008. www.alternet.org/blogs/rights/77296.

Sharon Begley, Anne Underwood, and Mary Carmichael, "The Anatomy of Violence," *Newsweek,* April 30, 2007.

Shaoni Bhattacharya, "Violence May Be a 'Socially Infectious Disease,'" *New Scientist,* May 27, 2005.

Brady Campaign to Prevent Gun Violence, "Guns in Colleges

and Schools? The Gun Lobby Is Threatening School Safety," 2008. www.bradycampaign.org/action/schools/.

Edwin C. Darden, "Safe from Harm," *American School Board Journal*, December 2006.

Bill Dedman, "10 Myths About School Shootings," MSNBC.com, October 7, 2007. www.msnbc.msn.com/id/15111438.

Naomi Dillon, "A Measured Approach: After a Series of Deadly Shootings, Experts Urge Schools to Take Thoughtful Steps to Ensure Safety," *American School Board Journal*, December 2006.

Benjamin Dowling-Sendor, "When Child's Play Turns Tragic," *American School Board Journal*, June 2006.

Steven Dowshen, "Should You Worry About School Violence?" TeensHealth, February 2008. http://kidshealth.org/teen/school_jobs/bullying/school_violence.html.

Scott Elliot, "Is There Any Way to Stop a School Shooting?" *Dayton (OH) Daily News*, April 17, 2007.

Trent England and Steve Muscatello, "Common Sense on School Violence," *San Diego Union-Tribune*, April 21, 2005.

James Alan Fox, "Topics in University Security: Lockdown 101," *New York Times*, April 16, 2008.

Alan Gottlieb and Dave Workman, "The Dirty Little Secret of 'Gun-Free School Zones,'" *Hawaii Reporter*, December 26, 2006. www.hawaiireporter.com/story.aspx?115ec9d8-8c23-486a-8d12-a381c01822ef.

Corinne Gregory and Lisa Finan, "Dealing with the School Bully Epidemic," AlterNet, May 19, 2008. www.alternet.org/story/85731/dealing_with_the_school_bully_epidemic.

Ken Hanson, "The Uncomfortable Truth About School Shootings," Buckeye Firearms Association, October 4, 2006. www. buckeyefirearms.org/modules.php?name=News&file= article&sid=3311.

Joanne Jacobs, "It Isn't the Bullying, Stupid, It's the Parenting: Don't Blame School Shootings on Kids Being Bullied," Reason Foundation, December 4, 2007. www.reason.org/commentaries/ jacobs_20071204.shtml.

Patrick Jonston, "Stop School Shootings: Let Teachers Carry Guns," NewsWithViews.com, October 8, 2006. www.newswith views.com/Johnston/patrick4.htm.

Gil Klein, "No Child Left Behind Not Working to Combat School Violence," J.R. Roberts Security Strategies, April 14, 2005. www.jrrobertssecurity.com/security-news/security-crime-news0062.htm.

Jeffrey Kluger, Barbara Kiviat, and Alice Park, "Why They Kill," *Time*, April 30, 2007.

Dave Kopel, "Defending Our Schools," National Rifle Association Institute for Legislative Action, January 11, 2007. www. nraila.org//Issues/Articles/Read.aspx?ID=228.

Alice Mathias, "Fear and Learning on Campus," *New York Times*, April 16, 2008.

Neal McCluskey, "Violence in Public Schools: A Dirty Secret," *School Reform News*, June 2005.

Kate McGreevy, "School Violence Is Under-Reported," *School Reform News*, April 1, 2005.

Reggie Moody, "Schools Can Cut School Violence, If They Still Have the Will," *Madison (WI) Capital Times*, January 29, 2007.

MSNBC.com, "Wisconsin Lawmaker Wants Teachers to Carry Guns," October 5, 2006. www.msnbc.msn.com/id/15142930.

National School Safety and Security Services, "Persistently Dangerous Schools: School Safety Implications of No Child Left Behind Law's 'Persistently Dangerous Schools' Definition." www.schoolsecurity.org/trends/persistently_dangerous.html.

———, "School Crime Reporting and School Crime Under-reporting." www.schoolsecurity.org/trends/school_crime_ reporting .html.

National Youth Violence Prevention Resource Center, "School Violence," April 18, 2008. www.safeyouth.org/scripts/topics/ school.asp.

New York Times, "School Shootings and Violence," Topics, February 15, 2008. http://topics.nytimes.com/top/reference/ timestopics/subjects/s/school_shootings/index.html.

Will Okun, "Policing the Halls," *New York Times*, December 6, 2007.

Bill Redeker, "Surviving a School Shooting," ABC News, April 17, 2007. http://abcnews.go.com/US/story?id=3050247.

Ken Schwartz, "Packing Heat in Lecture," BusinessToday.org, March 1, 2006. www.businesstoday.org/index.php?option=com _content&task=view&id=205&Itemid=43.

Brian J. Siebel and Allen K. Rostron, "No Gun Left Behind: The Gun Lobby's Campaign to Push Guns into Colleges and Schools," Brady Center to Prevent Gun Violence, May 2007. www.brady campaign.org/xshare/pdf/reports/no-gun-left-behind.pdf.

Stacy A. Teicher, "How Students Can Break the 'Code of Silence,'" *Christian Science Monitor*, October 19, 2006.

Greg Toppo, "High-Tech School Security Is on the Rise," *USA Today*, October 10, 2006.

———, "Keeping School Violence at Bay," *USA Today*, June 27, 2004.

———, "School Violence Hits Lower Grades," *USA Today*, January 12, 2003.

Susan Troller, "Facing School Violence," *Madison (WI) Capital Times*, January 11, 2007.

Gerard Valentino, "The False Hope of Gun-Free School Zones," Buckeye Firearms Association, December 16, 2004. www. buck eyefirearms.org/article1997.html.

Irene Van der Zande, "Violence in Schools: Helping Children Feel Empowered in the Face of Armed Violence in Schools," Kidpower.org. www.kidpower.org/ARTICLES/weapons-in-schools.html.

Paul Joseph Watson and Alex Jones, "Campus Gun Ban Disarmed Virginia Victims," PrisonPlanet.com, April 16, 2007. www.prison planet.com/articles/april2007/160407gunban.htm.

Wheeling (WV) Intelligencer , "Keeping Order in the Classroom," January 19, 2008.

Walter Williams, "Dealing with School Violence," *Capitalism Magazine*, July 6, 2003.

Bill Zalud, "School Violence: How Bad Is It?" *Security Magazine*, November 20, 2006.